GOD IS MY INSTRUCTOR PILOT

by Alan H. Conklin

Printed by
PARACLETE PRESS

God is My Instructor Pilot

© 2001 by Conklin & de Decker, Orleans, MA 02653

ISBN: 0-9666787-1-0

First Edition—November, 2001

Printed in the U.S.A.

Contents

Foreword

ALAN H. CONKLIN has been involved with airplanes, one way or another, for nearly all of his life. His experiences in both the military and civilian sectors of aviation are interesting on a personal level and significant on an historic level.

God is My Instructor Pilot is a factual account of Mr. Conklin's life-long aviation experiences. It is an engaging personal account, beginning with his early introduction to flying, up through his significant involvement in commercial aviation history. Of particular interest to me is his involvement with the United States Air Force and the unselfish contributions he made in helping to defend our country as a military pilot.

The experiences of Al Conklin as an Air Force pilot were varied and noteworthy. In the late 1940s, he was assigned to Alaska, flying the Aleutian Island chain through bitter cold Arctic skies and snow storms. His aircraft was the renowned C-47 "Sky train," more commonly known as the "Gooney Bird." The Gooney Bird, also known in civilian circles as the Douglas DC-3, is one of the great classic American aircraft of all times. Mr. Conklin's mastery of this famed aircraft in the wilds of Alaska lends to both engaging and entertaining reading.

The author devotes several chapters of God is My Instructor Pilot to his service and participation in the Korean War. In it, he flew another classic American cargo plane, the Fairchild C-119 "Boxcar." First he writes of his efforts, along with his fellow Air

Force C-119 pilots, to fly these airborne carriers to the Korean war zone by way of the vast Pacific Ocean. Flying the Pacific in a C-119 in the early 1950s was not a simple non-stop flight. It involved multiple island hopping through both beautiful and horrid weather conditions to reach Japan, the staging area of U.S. Air Force participation in the early stages of the Korean War. Then he describes his intense involvement in the war itself, in and around the massive combat encounters on the ground. His role as a military cargo pilot was to provide logistical support to the troops on the front line during times that included the most intensive ground fighting.

The Korean War is often referred to as the "forgotten War." This does not mean that U.S. Military contributions in Korea were any less involved or any less intense than American efforts in World War II just a few years prior. Students of history remember America's role in the great Berlin Airlift in 1948, but in the "forgotten war" of Korea, few remember the equally valiant efforts of American pilots played in providing airlift support to American and other United Nations troops. The only significant difference is that this flying effort was accomplished under actual, not threatened, combat conditions. This book educates the reader of these efforts. As this book was written, America is celebrating the 50th anniversary of the Korean War. It is time that Americans and others had the opportunity to learn more about the patriotic efforts of the men who participated in this war.

Al Conklin has been successful in his aviation efforts throughout his life. He admits that his life involvement with airplanes was interesting and personally rewarding. Yet, he takes little credit for his successes. Instead, he attributes his accomplishments to God. He feels that God was with him all the way. His steadfast faith and his unwavering commitment to God and his country has resulted in this occasion whereby he can proudly tell his story in the pages of this inspiring book.

Jerry Rep
Air Force Museum Foundation Editor/Publisher

God is My Instructor Pilot

ALL MY ADULT LIFE I have been a typical, pragmatic professional pilot. First as an Air Force pilot, for almost 10 years, and then as an aircraft salesman selling business and corporate aircraft. Early on, I read Colonel Bob Scott's excellent book entitled *God is My Copilot* and, being the self-centered person that I am, actually agreed with the good Colonel that He was in that right seat and often helped me when the flying got rough. I was in charge, but He was there to help me.

I remember one November afternoon in 1949, while stationed with the Air Force on Adak in the Aleutian Islands. I was flying left seat in a C-47 (Gooney Bird) on an IFR flight (every flight in the Aleutians was Instrument Flight Rules) from Cold Bay to Cape Air Force Base on Umnak. The weather was poor when we departed, but not unusual, and was solid instruments the whole route. I was a route check pilot, an instructor pilot, and occupying the right seat was Lt. East our very competent Base Operations Officer. So what was there to worry about?

One of the rules for flying IFR in the Aleutians in those days, because of the unusual weather, was that you had to have two alternate airports beyond your destination, rather than the stateside requirement of just one. Our two alternates for that trip were Adak and Shemya, about 425 miles beyond Adak. The weather behind us was deteriorating and the barometer was dropping rapidly at Shemya. As we cruised along, the weather began to rapidly and seriously deteriorate, initially behind us and then ahead of us. First, Cold Bay went below minimums and after we were well past Dutch Harbor, Umnak (our planned destination) went to 400 foot overcast and 2 miles visibility. Adak was holding up at 1500 feet and seven miles, so we elected to pass Umnak and go on to Adak. Interesting, but not of any great concern.

Then, ahead of us Shemya, our second alternate, went below minimums and as we got closer to Adak, it started to deteriorate as well. Everything behind us was closed and everything beyond Adak was now closed, leaving us with no option except to get into Adak. By the time we arrived over Adak, the weather was rapidly deteriorating with heavy wet snow falling. Happily, we had a first class GCA (Ground Controlled Approach—radar) team to help bring us in. And bring us in they must, because we had no place else to go. To add a little more excitement to the situation, there was only one runway we could land on at Adak and it had a 25 knot tailwind, with gusts to 35. Oh yes, and by this time it was dark outside. This was the kind of day we earned our flying pay.

We reported in to Approach Control over the high cone of Adak's low frequency range station and started our normal instrument approach. GCA would monitor our initial approach and then pick us up over Zito Point and bring us in the rest of the way. Aside from the wind blowing the wrong way, the initial approach went well and GCA picked us up and started us down the glide slope using their precision radar. About halfway down the glide slope, the GCA controller advised us to pull up and go around because they had lost us in the snow clutter on their radarscope.

So we picked up our landing gear and climbed back up to the high cone to start our second approach. Everything was routine so far, but I was getting concerned over the still rapidly deteriorating weather at Adak. Everything went according to the book until we were on the final approach a second time and once again GCA told us they couldn't follow us in the heavy snow clutter on their precision radar. Pull up and go around for a third try. This time they suggested not using the precision radar on final approach, but that they would give us heading information using their non-precision search radar and provide us with the altitude we *should* be at as they gave us the headings we needed.

Having already made two attempts down that final approach I pretty well had the power and attitude in mind needed to fly the proper glide slope. And it was a good thing too, because the heavy wet snow had frozen up our pitot tubes, that fed our airspeed meters, and we now had no airspeed indication. GCA was able to follow us better in the snow with their search radar. About a half mile off the end of the runway, radar told us that they had lost us for a third time. I held my power and attitude steady for just a little longer, because I knew we had to get our bird on the deck fast or we weren't to get it down at all. At about 500 feet Lt. East yelled that he could make out the glow of the runway Bartow lights through the precipitation. I looked up and he was right. I could see the runway lights through the heavy snow that was falling. That was the good news. The bad news was that the tailwind down the runway had pushed us too far down the runway for us to land on this pass.

To understand our predicament you have to visualize runway 23 at Davis AFB. On the right side, just off the edge of the runway, was a small hill that had been partially bulldozed away to make room for the runway. It was probably 150 feet high. Beyond that were higher hills and then Mt. Moffett, an extinct volcano, about 4,000 feet high. On the left side, at the approach end of the runway, was another small hill with family quarters for Navy personnel. Beyond that was the Air Force base and Sweeper Cove. Sweeper Cove is an arm off of Kuluk Bay and the Navy's port facility for Adak. Behind us was the 25 mile expanse of Kuluk Bay and ahead of us were more mountains. We had less than 500 feet of ceiling and less than 1/2 mile of visibility in that heavy wet snow. I dropped our altitude to 300 feet.

I elected to fly a low visibility pattern by making a 180 degree left turn around the Navy quarters and out over Kuluk Bay, flying straight ahead for two minutes and then a second 180 degree left turn which, normally, should put us right in line with the runway once again. All this was on instruments because of the poor visibility, at night, over Kuluk Bay. We completed the pattern okay, but the strong tailwind down runway 23 loused me up and once again I was pushed too far down the runway to land. So, around we went again and this time I really stretched the pattern out over the Bay, with no visual reference to the ground, and found myself lined up with the runway okay, but still high.

But I had had enough. I pushed the wheel forward, planted the main gear on the runway and really started working the brakes to slow us down. The only trouble was that the heavy snow gave us no traction and we just kept sliding along, helped, of course, by the strong tailwind. Suddenly the right wheel hit a bare spot on the runway and that caused us to swerve to the right, out through the plowed snow bank to the side of the runway and through several of the runway Bartow lights. By jazzing the right engine I got the C-47 turned back to the left, but over- controlled it slightly and it was once again back through the Bartow lights, the snow bank and we finally came to a halt a few hundred feet short of the end of the runway.

I told John East to call the tower and have them send out a tug to tow us into the flight line, which they did. I was too wiped out to even taxi that bird back to the barn, particularly with a strong wind blowing. And, then, God and I sat back and relaxed after a couple of hours of tough flying together. He sure was with me that night.

There is a world of difference, in the flying business, between an instructor pilot and a copilot. They both, normally, will ride in the right-hand seat when in the cockpit and the regular pilot manipulating the controls will fly in the left-hand seat. The instructor is the experienced old hand and is either teaching or checking the person flying in the left seat. The instructor is always in charge. The copilot is generally the inexperienced fellow who is just learning the ropes from the regular pilot. There is a world of difference in status between the two.

It wasn't until a relatively few years ago, after my wife, Martha, and I had moved to a Christian community on Cape Cod, that I recognized my arrogance toward God. I had always known that he was there in the cockpit with me—incidentally, I have never found an atheist in the cockpit yet—but I always figured that I was in charge. How wrong I was all those years. I know now that He was always in charge and guiding me all the way.

As I look back on my adult life I can see his hand in everything I ever did and how it has all fit together. He was leading me all the way. For example, I took twin-engine advanced training at Pampa Air Force Base in Texas and I stayed on as an instructor. While there I was sent to Col. Joe Duckworth's Instrument Instructors School to learn precision instrument flying. I shortly became one of Col. Joe's instructors. This experience with precision instrument flying was what helped me that wild night on Adak and also when flying the Korean Airlift later on. It was at Col. Joe's school that I learned about flying on instruments using power and attitude to maintain airspeed that helped me when we lost our airspeed indications at Adak.

Col. Joe Duckworth did more to save aircraft and flight crews during the war than any other single person. Aside from those of us who worked for him, very few people have ever heard of him. To me he is one of my great heroes and was a big influence on my professional life. I'm sure he was part of my Instructor Pilot's plan for me.

After I got out of the Air Force, my first big boss in business aviation was Carl Wooton at Aero Commander in Oklahoma City. Carl was a very active Christian and never failed to open a marketing meeting with a prayer—the only V.P. of Marketing that I have ever seen do this. I remember going to talk with Carl one time with some kind of a problem and never forgot his answer. He said "Al, you just do the best job you know how and the good Lord will take care of all the rest." It has always worked.

I remember a number of years back when I felt I had to take an unpopular stand, against our senior management, in favor of a couple of my customers. I didn't get fired, but was reassigned from new aircraft sales to used aircraft sales with the idea that I would end up resigning. It almost worked and I was actively looking for another job. However, two things happened to change my mind. First, we got a new president for our company who I instantly liked. I liked his basic philosophies for running our company and he had ideas to make our used aircraft department grow. Second, we had a major recession in our business and customers almost stopped buying new aircraft and bought used ones instead. Our used aircraft sales never even slowed down. I made enough commission money for us to move to our Christian community on Cape Cod a couple of years later and start our own company. God was still in charge. He knew where I was supposed to be working at that time, even though, at first, I didn't see it. My initial reaction to being demoted to selling used aircraft was that I had gotten a kick in the tail, but it turned out to be a real blessing in disguise.

The Air Corps

1942 TO 1946

THE OTHER DAY A YOUNG MAN came to talk with us about making a career in the aviation business. It got me to thinking a little about how I had gotten started and the fun I've had over these past 61 years of being involved with aircraft. It has never been dull!

I got my pilot's license while at Lehigh University in 1940, courtesy of Uncle Sam's Civil Pilot Training Program (CPTP). We were not in WW II yet, but the handwriting was on the wall and our government was foresighted enough to build a large pool of trained pilots through this civilian flight training program, largely organized at colleges and universities all around the country. We flew with Lehigh Valley Aircraft at Allentown-Bethlehem Airport (ABE) in eastern Pennsylvania.

Airplanes always fascinated me. My older brother Steward, taught me the intricacies of building gliders and rubber band powered flying models and I couldn't wait to become an Air Force pilot. Upon graduating from Lehigh, I was commissioned a Second Lieutenant in the Infantry and went on active duty. I quickly applied for, and got, a transfer as a Student Officer to Air Force Pilot Training.

In 1942-43 pilot training was a most interesting experience. The Army Air Corps was exploding from about 900 pilots to

25,000 pilots a year and things tended to be a little wild. I came on active duty as a Second Lieutenant in the Infantry. As soon as I checked into my first assignment at Camp Wheeler I went to my Commanding Officer, explained my flying training during my junior and senior years at Lehigh University and that I'd like to transfer to the Army Air Corps. He laughed at my thought and said it would be OK with him except no one had been transferred out of Camp Wheeler in the two years he had been there.

He endorsed my request, but said it wouldn't do any good. What neither of us knew was that a telegram had come a couple of days before that said the Air Corps needed pilots urgently and that anyone that wanted to apply should be expedited. As soon as the word got out, there were a bunch of other requests sent in and ten days later three of us from my battalion were on our way to Kelly Field at San Antonio, TX. At San Antonio Aviation Cadet Center (SAACC) we were assigned to the one flight of Student Officers. All the rest were Aviation Cadets. The officers were segregated into one flight, but other than that, did everything that the cadets were required to do.

Our Flight Leader was Capt. Billy B. Beardon, a most interesting guy. Until he joined us at SAACC he had been General George Patton's aide. Patton had sent him there to become his personal pilot. He was one tough cookie and knew all the regulations inside out. I remember one night when our flight had blinker light code practice on our big parade ground. When we were finished, Beardon formed us up and we proceeded to march back to our barracks. That night the cadets were also practicing interior guard duty and were patrolling each block with a sentry carrying a rifle. So on each block we were stopped by a cadet, doing guard duty, with the challenge, "Halt! Who is there?" Bill would answer that we were Blank Flight.

The cadet guard was then supposed to say, "Advance *one* to be recognized." After a few blocks Beardon was getting a little annoyed at this monotonous procedure. Then we ran into a cadet who got a little confused, when confronted by a whole flight of 32

Primary School at Hicks Field, Texas. Capt. Fletcher, me, our instructor, Pop Reeves, Lt. Smith and a/c Saryendarion.

officers, and told Beardon, 'Advance and be recognized." Billy never even hesitated and gave us the order, "Column of files from the right. March!" After a bunch of us had paraded past this totally confused cadet, Beardon yelled, "Charge!" and we all ran past the startled guard and the remaining few guards between us and our barracks.

At Preflight School Martha and I bought our first car. In my junior year in ROTC at Lehigh I had purchased my dress uniform. Shortly after going on active duty we were given a $150 "uniform allowance." In San Antonio we took that allowance and bought a '36 Plymouth for $125. It served us well all during the war.

After Preflight School at SAACC six of us student officers went to Hicks Field, a few miles north of Ft. Worth, TX, for Primary School. Primary School was a piece of cake for me, because it was essentially a repeat of what I had learned in my CPTP course at Lehigh. Also, I was very lucky (God's hand?) in being assigned to "Pop" Reeves as my instructor. "Pop" had formerly been an instructor in the CPTP so rather than waste my time teaching me what I already knew, spent his time polishing my techniques. The result was I got good grades on my check rides. I was most fortunate.

That was the good news. The bad news was that we had a Captain who was second in command of our little base. He had gone through pilot training as a cadet and didn't like student officers taking training. He saw my grades on the various stages (flying tests) in my training and commented that no one could get better grades than he had gotten when he went through Primary School. He also stated that he was going to give me a check ride and no matter how good I did I was going to flunk the ride. My civilian Group Commander warned me what was coming up and not to be surprised. This was not a good morale booster for me. However, before this Captain could give me my check ride, he was suddenly called home on an emergency leave and didn't return in time to give me that predetermined ride.

The Student Officers did everything the cadets did, but with minor changes. For example, we took calisthenics at the same time they did, except we led the calisthenics relieving the regular officers of that chore. We also covered the job of Officer of the Day (OD) relieving the regular officers of that chore also. This was a big help to them, as there were only three of them, if I remember correctly. Everyone else was a civilian. One of our Student Officers was Lt. Smith who was commissioned in the Armored Corps and always bragged about how well he knew his weapons. One day he was OD and had to go flying which meant that he had to leave his OD arm band, cap and 45 cal. pistol at operations. While he was up, Captain Fletcher and I field-stripped his pistol and dumped all the parts into his cap. When Smitty picked up his gear after flying, he couldn't reassemble the pistol. He was used to field stripping his pistol and laying the various parts out in sequence and then reassembling it in reverse order. With just a pile of parts he couldn't figure it out. A couple of Infantry Officers, with great glee, showed this "expert" how to do it.

After Primary School, all the student officers went to Randolph Field for our Basic Training where we formed Flight A,

Squadron R of Class 43 E. There were a few holes in our Flight from guys like Fletcher and Smitty who had washed out in Primary school. Going to Randolph Field (The West Point of the Air) had always been the one big ambition in my life and I had made it. But just barely, because ours was the last class to graduate from Basic training there. After we left it became an Instructors School.

My real alma mater. The "West Point of the air."

At Randolph we were introduced to the North American BT-14, Basic Trainer. The BT14 was the most difficult flying transition I ever encountered. For the first time I had to deal with adjustable pitch propellers and wing flaps and other big airplane equipment. We also got our first taste of night flying and formation flying. After the BT-14, all other aircraft were a piece of cake to fly.

I had an excellent instructor at Randolph. Several classes before us he had had a student who was always getting airsick. Using a little psychology, he told that student there was one sure way to prevent airsickness and that was to take an orange, cut a hole in the top and then suck out the juice just before he went flying. It worked and the kid went on to graduate with no more airsickness.

All went well with this thankful student until he found himself flying a B-17 in the Eighth Air Force in England, where there were no oranges during the war. Every month my instructor was faithfully sending his former student a crate of oranges in order to keep him flying. That's real dedication.

Martha and I lived off base in the little town of New Braunfels, about 15 miles north of Randolph. Here we shared a house with Grover and Frieda Nelson. One time Grover and I were both on a cross country flight and didn't get back to Randolph until fairly late. We knew that the gals would have long since had their dinner, so we stopped at a butcher shop, in town, to pick up a nice thick steak to broil for our dinner (this was before meat rationing). At this point in time, Texans had no idea how to cook anything except Mexican food or chicken fried steak. When we told the butcher to cut a nice one inch thick steak, he gave us a funny look and seriously asked us if we were going to roast it. The Texans learned a lot about how to eat from the Yankees stationed there during the war. Ice cream was really ice water and there was almost nothing in the way of baked goods to choose from. Of course, all that has changed, but even today I can't stand the idea of a chicken fried steak.

After Basic we went to Pampa Army Airfield way up in the Panhandle of Texas, about 55 miles northeast of Amarillo. Pampa was a real cultural shock to Martha and I, who had been brought up in a suburban New York environment. There was one small hotel, a couple of cafes (not restaurants) and a couple of filling stations. We arrived on the same day as the class at Pampa AAF was graduating. There was no room for us at the hotel. However, they took pity on us—we had been driving all day—and set up a bed in an empty salesman's show room.

Pampa AAF was an advanced twin-engine training field. It was very spartan with all buildings just tarpaper covered, single story frame shacks set on concrete blocks. The three hangars were pretty nice, as was the Production Line Maintenance (PLM) hangar. We also had three nice asphalt runways. Instruction was good and flown in Cessna UC-78s—The Bamboo Bomber—and in the terrific Curtiss AT-9. The UC-78 was adapted from a Cessna commercial aircraft. The AT-9 was an all-metal, on-purpose designed, twin-engine trainer. Its one big drawback was its all-metal construction at a time when aluminum was in short supply. The AT-9 was intended to be a transition trainer into the twin engine P-38 fighter. However, I had one P-38 pilot tell me that it really should have been the other way around, with the P-38 used to transition into the AT-9. Once I was shown how to properly fly it, I really liked the airplane.

Keep in mind that in early 1943 the Army Air Corps was growing by leaps and bounds. It was in a state of radical transition. Our instructors did the best they knew how, but their technical knowledge was very limited. When flying on instruments we learned to fly needle-ball-airspeed and were not permitted to use the gyro stabilized artificial horizon or the directional gyrocompass. When we asked why, we were told that they were not reliable. Four months later at Joe Duckworth's Instrument School we learned differently. When flying the AT-9 we were told, "Don't ever let your airspeed get below 120 mph, and with only half flaps, on the final approach for landing. When we asked why, the response was the standard answer of, "You'll kill yourself." Two months later, at the instructor's school, they really taught us how to fly power off, full flap landings, in the same aircraft, safely at 90 mph. The Air Corps was that quickly learning how to fly their airplanes.

When I was learning the intricacies of single engine procedures, I was told never to turn toward the dead engine. When I asked why, I was told the stock answer of, "You'll kill yourself." Our instructors at Pampa had never been told about the aerodynamics of "minimum single engine control speed." As long as you have that speed you can even do acrobatics with one engine inoperative.

To give you an indication of how rapidly things were changing in flight training in early 1943, three of us former Student Officers—Jim Fox, Barney Hooton and I—were sent to the new Instructors School at Randolph Field as soon as we got our pilots wings in May 1943. Two months before we had been there when it was a Basic School. At this new school they really taught us how to safely fly a twin-engine airplane. We learned maximum performance takeoffs and landings (taught by Jimmy Doolittle to his Tokyo Raiders so they could fly their twin-engine bombers off an aircraft carrier), single engine control speed, so that we could safely turn into or away from that dead engine and all the other radical techniques unknown to our instructors back at Pampa.

Lt. Reilly was our instructor at Randolph Field. Just before Jim Fox and I were to return to Pampa (Barney Hooton was held over one class because of a sprained ankle playing volleyball), we were called in by Reilly for a briefing. He warned us that we would have difficulty teaching these new techniques on our return, because it was so alien to what they were teaching based on their limited knowledge. He simply asked us to do the best we could.

When Jim and I got back we were each given three students and we were in the same Flight under 1st Lt. Andy Anderson. We proceeded to teach our cadets the new techniques. It was easy to spot our cadets in the traffic pattern. The other students started their descent to landings miles out from the runway. They made power-on approaches at 120 mph and with half flaps. Our cadets would hold altitude to about 1/2 of a mile out, cut their power, use full flaps and come down at a very steep angle at 90 mph.

One day I came into operations and Jimmy Fox was on the carpet in front of Andy. Andy had just given one of Jim's students a check ride. On the downwind leg of the traffic pattern at an auxiliary field, Andy had cut the left engine (on the side towards the field) and told him to make an emergency landing. The student completed his downwind leg and turned ninety degrees to the left (into the dead engine) and at the correct time made a second left turn to line up with the runway, put down half flaps and at 90 mph made a good approach to the runway. Just before they touched down, Andy fired up the dead engine and they headed back to the home field. Andy was good in that he didn't chew out the student, but did ask him why he had turned twice into the dead engine. The student said that Lt. Fox had taught him that and why—it was better to make two left hand 90 degree turns, during which he could keep his field in sight, than to make two 270 degree right hand turns where he could not keep the field in sight.

It was right after this incident that I walked in and joined the discussion with Jim and Andy. The net result was that Andy said that it was OK for us to teach these new techniques if we wanted to (although he thought it was very risky) but for check rides they must fly the old way. Jimmy went home and was furious. He wrote to Barney (still at Randolph) what was going on and how frustrating it all was. Barney showed the letter to Lt. Reilly, our instructor there, and he asked for the letter. Reilly assured Barney that he would delete any names. Within 10 days a Standardization Board from Randolph arrived at Pampa and they rode with every pilot on the base, including Col. Campbell our Base Commander, except for Jim Fox and myself. From then on we all taught by the new rules. This was an exciting time in the flying business. Lots of changes.

While all of this was going on, Bailey Henderson, Wade Dryer, Chris Eastin and Bern Logan were sent to Col. Joe Duckworth's Instrument Instructors School at Bryan, TX. Their job was to learn about this new, full panel, precision method of flying on instruments. Upon their return to Pampa they formed a special Instrument Training Squadron with instructors that would do nothing but teach instrument flying. This was a radical change in the curriculum, but Col. Campbell assured us that if any of us wanted out at the end of the first class to go back to teaching regular flying, we would be obliged. None of us ever did.

Shortly after joining the Instrument Squadron, Jim Fox, Lt. Marshburn and I were sent to Bryan AAF to the Instrument Instructors School. Col. Joe's school had a profound effect on my professional flying career. I really learned how to fly precision instruments and once Bryan was in my records, I always became an instrument check pilot and this earned me special privileges. It also prepared me to fly in real weather, later on, in the Aleutian Islands. The Aleutian weather is generally considered to be the

The ring leaders of our Instrument Squadron (V) at Pampa, Texas. Bailey Henderson, Wade Dryer, Chris Eastin and Bern Logan.

worst in the world. And, once again, an indication of God's hand in my life.

It would be a fascinating statistic to know how many of us former AF crew members are alive today thanks to the efforts of one little known AF Colonel named Joe Duckworth. Back in 1943, Joe was a civilian and personal friend of Gen. "Hap" Arnold, Air Corps Chief of Staff. Joe was then VP Operations of American Airlines. Early in 1943 he walked into "Hap's" office and said, "I hear you are losing more bombers to weather than you are to enemy action." "Hap" acknowledged the problem and Joe said, "I can solve your problem, and fast, if you will give me three things. "Hap," knowing Joe, was intrigued and wanted to know what those three things were. Joe said, "One, I want first priority on people. Two, I want first priority on equipment and three, leave me alone." "Hap" listened to the rest of his plan, gave him his three wishes and promptly commissioned him a Colonel in the Air Corps.

The first thing Col. Joe did was go to Air Corps Personnel and pick three company grade pilots who had formerly been college professors. The four of them moved to Randolph Field near San Antonio, TX and set up shop in a room in a temporary barracks there. It was right next to the barracks that I was in attending the brand new Advanced Instructors School. It wasn't until a few months later that I found out what this little group of four pilots was doing.

Col. Joe was teaching them full-panel, precision instrument flying using all the instruments—including the Artificial Horizon and Directional Gyro. Up to this time the Air Corps didn't want us to use these two gyro-stabilized instruments because "they could tumble and, therefore, were unreliable." Col. Joe would ride with one of his charges while the other two would make a buddy ride. They would fly one half the day and the other half was spent writing the new course syllabus. When they were finished each of his professors took three students and ran them through the course. Then those nine took three and soon they had a cadre for their Instrument Instructors School.

In the meantime, Col. Joe had lined up Bryan Air Force Base for the school and new AT-6s for trainers. He wanted us to learn how to cope with the torque of a single-engine plane. He also lined up the latest avionics to be installed in these trainers. ADFs (radio compass) were installed that at that time were common in bombers, but not normally found in a trainer. Also installed was a new thing called an ILS (Instrument Landing System). In 1943 all the ground based ILS systems were being sent to the combat theaters. Two were to be found in the United States—one at Wright Field for test purposes and the other at Bryan for Duckworth's Instrument Instructor Program.

By early summer of 1943 Col. Joe's Instrument Instructors School was in business and was bringing in small groups of pilots from Air Bases all around the world. They were taught the new full panel method of instrument flying, then sent back to their home base to teach the new system back there. To one of the very first classes at Bryan, Pampa sent Capt. Bailey Henderson and two of his fellow instructors. When they returned, they formed something new for an Advanced Flying School. It was called an Instrument Squadron and was in addition to the four regular Contact Squadrons. Jim Fox and I returned from Randolph Field and taught one class of Contact Flying when we were drafted into Bailey Henderson's new Instrument Squadron.

Bailey's plan was to rotate each of the four contact squadrons, one at a time, for two weeks of concentrated full-panel instrument training. When we were first sent to this new Instrument Squadron, Col. Danny Campbell, our Base Commander, assured us we only had to stay for one class and if we didn't like the assignment he would arrange for us to be sent back to teaching contact flying again. I don't remember anyone asking to be sent back. At the end of that first class, Pampa sent 120 newly rated pilots out into the Air Corps fully qualified on full-panel instrument flying. It was part of what Joe Duckworth had in mind when he told "Hap" Arnold that he would change the Air Corp's instrument flying skills fast.

In July 1943 British pilots were also being trained in the new instrument techniques of instrument flying at Bryan AAF. On the 27th of July, Bryan was alerted that a hurricane was coming ashore at Galveston, TX and that their planes would likely have to be evacuated. Many of these English pilots were "Aces" from battles in the air over Europe. They felt that they deserved to be trained in the top fighters used by the United States and not in the AT-6 trainers used at Bryan. When they heard about flying these trainers away from the storm, they hard-timed their instructors about the frailty of the AT-6. The problem was that few Europeans had ever experienced a real hurricane. They thought it was just a big thunderstorm.

Finally, Col. Joe had enough of the ribbing and whining of these British pilots and bet them that he could fly one of our AT-6s into the storm and back to prove that both the plane and his instrument flying technique were sound. The bet was on and a highball to the winner. Col. Duckworth looked across the breakfast table at Lt. Ralph O'Hair, the only navigator on the field that morning, and asked him to fly with him. O'Hair was taken back by the bet, but agreed to fly with him, due to his respect for Duckworth's skill as a pilot.

Since they felt that headquarters wouldn't approve the flight due to the risk to the plane and crew, they decided to make the flight without authorization. The main problem that passed through Lt. O'Hair's mind was that if their single engine quit for some reason, like being flooded out by the heavy rain, they would be in deep trouble. As they closed in on the storm at a height of between four thousand and nine thousand feet the air became very turbulent. O'Hair described the flight now as like, "being tossed like a stick in a dog's mouth." The rain was very heavy as they flew through the darkness fighting the updrafts and the downdrafts.

Suddenly they broke out into the calm eye of the storm. It was not the original purpose of the flight, but really an accident. It must be remembered that no one had ever flown through a hurricane before. The sky was filled with bright clouds and it seemed like they were surrounded by a shower-curtain of darker clouds. As they looked down they could see the countryside. The storm had indeed moved inland. O'Hair described the shape of the center of the storm as like a leaning cone. The lower section was dragging a bit behind due to the friction from contact with the land. The eye seemed to be nine to ten miles across as they circled inside. As they exited the eye, the dark overcast and rain again pounded the plane until they made their way out of the storm and headed back towards Bryan AFB. When they arrived back at the field, the weather officer, Lt. William Jones-Burdick, asked to be flown into the storm. So, O'Hair jumped out of the back seat and the weather officer jumped in and flew off into the hurricane with Col. Duckworth.

That night the bet was paid and no more comments were given regarding the sturdiness of the AT-6 trainers. That was also the last flight into a hurricane for Lt. O'Hair. (As recalled by Lt. Col. (Retired) Ralph O'Hair). Bryan Field went on to be the Mecca for

Allied Pilots wanting to learn more about the fine art of precision instrument flying. Also, Col. Duckworth soon had a belly tank—for more range—installed on an AT-6 and whenever a hurricane popped up in the Carribean area he would fire up his long-range AT-6 and go fly through it—generally by himself. He was the first Hurricane Hunter. As he told us, his instructors, "The only way to really learn about flying in weather is to go fly in it." He was quite a guy and a real leader.

Not long after helping to start the new Instrument Squadron at Pampa, Jim Fox, Joe Marshburn and I were sent to Bryan to attend Joe Duckworth's Instrument Instructor School. Here we learned to use the new Instrument Landing System and to fly the complex "C" Pattern to less than 5 degrees of heading error, 5 mph in airspeed and 50 feet of altitude to become members of the Champagne Club. On my final night at Bryan, my wife called to tell me that she was in labor and going to the hospital to have our first baby.

The next morning I was rushed thru my final flight exam for the course and Col. Duckworth authorized the use of one of our specially equipped AT-6s and an instructor friend of mine to fly me back to Pampa. After landing we parked in front of Operations just as Col. Campbell—our Base Commander—drove up. He came over to look at this special AT-6 with all of its new-fangled avionics equipment. As I was showing him all these goodies, he suddenly realized that I was back early from Bryan, and not in the usual transportation. When he asked why, I told him that Martha had gone into the hospital to have our first child. He quickly bundled me into his staff car and had his driver deliver me to the hospital in town. In spite of all the delays, I got there before Chris was born, thanks to an assist from Col. Duckworth.

Danny Campbell was, without a doubt, the finest Base Commander I ever served under. He and his wife, Ruth, were well liked by everyone on the base. He was the only Base Commander that I was exposed to who didn't have, or need, a "Reserved for the CO" sign in the number one parking spot at Headquarters, the

One of our "loaded" AT-6 trainers. Note the ILS antenna in front of the windshield and Radio Compass loop behind the cockpit.

Officers Club or any place on the base. He didn't need one because no one would have thought to park in that spot. He was too well respected. When Dan moved on to fly B-17s, the new CO immediately had "Reserved for the CO" signs put up in all the appropriate spots. On the first day the one at the Officers Club got knocked down—by accident of course.

Pampa AAF was so well run, in fact, that they had the best maintenance record in our Command and was picked for the first training base to get B-25s for advanced twin-engine trainers when they became available. This was a surprise to Col. Howell M. Estes at Lubbock AAF who was so sure that the B-25s were going to Lubbock that he had already sent a number of his top instructors to B-25 transition schools. To make a long story short, in the fall of 1944 the already trained instructors at Lubbock were traded for an equal number of top instructors at Pampa. Most of us in the trade even swapped houses and Martha, Chris and I found ourselves in Lubbock, TX.

Because of my instrument training background, I was put in charge of the Link Trainer Department used to teach instrument procedures on the ground. Suddenly everything changed and instead of teaching cadets in twin-engine aircraft, we became a branch of Col. Joe Duckworth's Instrument Instructors School. With the exception of Col. Estes, our Base Commander, away went all pilots who had not graduated from Bryan, which if I remember correctly, were the Base Operations Officer and myself. Away went all the UC-78 and AT-10 trainers to be replaced by single-engine AT-6s with all the whistles and bells. What a change, and our Link Department suddenly increased to 20 Link Trainers. From one building to three. However, Tech Sergeant Harlan Fisk was up to the task, which was good for a greenhorn 1st Lt. like me.

Our department also was assigned the only twin-engine plane on the base. It was a nice clean C-45 Twin Beech. Its purpose was to give Link Trainer instructors familiarization rides in a real airplane to improve their skills working the Link trainers. It really amused me to have Col. Estes call me up to see if he could fly "my airplane." It sure beat an AT-6 for cross-country flying. And Col. Joe wanted us to get practical experience flying in weather.

Col. Joe Duckworth's training program had the second highest priority in the Air Corps. The only program with a higher priority

The Instrument Instructors School, Lubbock AAF, Texas. Sgt. Harlan Fisk and I discuss training procedures in our Link Trainer Department Office.

was the Manhattan Project—developing the atomic bomb. Anything we needed we got and this included unlimited cross-country privileges between classes. This was unheard of most places during the war and made our service more interesting.

One of the things we learned at Bryan was Long Range Cruise control for our aircraft. This was the same technique that Charles Lindbergh was teaching our fighter pilots in the Pacific. It was little known in the states. This extended the normal four-hour range of the AT-6 to six hours at a slightly reduced cruise speed. It effectively increased our max range by about 200 miles, or one- third. In 1943, there was also no such thing as a Green Instrument Card, in giving a qualified pilot his own Clearing Authority for flight. So Col. Joe gave each of his instructors a set of orders that permitted us to contact our Base Operations officer at Lubbock for a clearance. In essence it gave us our own clearing authority and a pretty handy arrangement to have in the early 1940s.

One time I was in Columbus, OH wanting to fly instrument weather to New York City with Boston as my alternate airport. It would require six hours of range in my AT-6. I filled out my Flight Plan and handed it to the Base Operations Officer for approval. He took one look at my proposed flight time and said, "No AT-6 has six hour of fuel aboard." I said that mine did and showed him my Form One from my flight into Columbus the night before, showing flight time and fuel consumed. He looked at the Form One and noted that my home base was Lubbock. He said, "Are you an instructor at Lubbock?" He then asked "Do you have a set of "those" orders with you." And I said that I did. He said, "OK, then I'll sign your clearance."

"Those" orders were an illustration of why Col. Duckworth told "Hap" Arnold that he wanted to be left alone. There was nothing in the regulations that covered that kind of situation. Col. Joe wanted us to get out and fly weather and push the envelope of the things we learned in his school. He knew that we would get resistance away from home base and this was one way to circumvent that resistance. It worked, but it was not exactly "by the book."

In "my book" I consider Col. Joe Duckworth to be one of the great, unsung heros of World War II. Single handedly he saved more aircraft and more flight crews than any person I have ever heard about. He quickly converted the Air Force from sloppy imprecise instrument flying to the Full Panel precise instrument flying that all pilots use today, whether flying a Cessna 172 or a Boeing 747. It is a shame that almost no one, except those of us who worked for him, have ever heard of Col. Joe Duckworth and the great things he did for our Air Force and our country.

Martha and I finished out World War II in Lubbock.

Robinson Aviation

1946 TO 1948

IN JANUARY 1946 THE WAR WAS OVER and we were relieved from active duty and returned home to Montclair, NJ. After a couple of false starts, I became the Parts Manager for Robinson Aviation at Teterboro Airport in New Jersey. Robinson Aviation, in those days, was a big Fixed Base Operator at Teterboro (TEB). We were the distributor for Aeronca, Culver and Stinson aircraft. We also had several dealers scattered around New Jersey. My job was to supply all the aircraft parts for Robinson and our dealers. I was not formally an aircraft salesman.

I do remember my first aircraft sale, however. After WW II small aircraft sold like crazy. During this time, the local Chrysler dealer (and a customer of ours) in Hackensack got the neat idea of displaying one of our Aeronca Champs in his showroom. A great idea for promoting both of our products. But to get our Champ into the car showroom necessitated removing its left wing. It was stored in my Parts Room at the airport.

During the post-war boom in aircraft sales, we had Aeroncas coming in by the trailer load—six to a trailer. We soon saturated the market and the bottom dropped out of aircraft sales. We had just taken delivery of two trailer loads and we had no customers for them. About this time one of our dealers called and told me he had damaged the left wing of one of his Champ trainers and could we get him one fast. He got the one in my Parts Room.

Before I ordered a replacement wing from the factory for our showroom bird, I got a wild idea. Why not sell the rest of the showroom Champ for parts. I put a pencil to the problem and discovered that if I sold all the struts, landing gear, windshield, engine and prop (all the rapidly moving parts) I could recoup our factory cost for the plane and reduce our aircraft inventory by one. The one item that bothered me was that I couldn't figure out how I'd ever sell the fuselage. Conventional wisdom said that if a plane was that badly damaged, it would be totaled. Management thought it was a good way to at least reduce our big inventory of aircraft and I was given an OK to sell the showroom Champ piece by piece. For many months that fuselage hung from the ceiling of my Parts Room and was often referred to as "Conklin's Folly."

Then one day I received a panicky call from our dealer near Asbury Park. One of his students had been a little low on his landing approach, hit a fence post and gutted the fuselage of his Champ. The rest of the plane was OK, but how much would a fuselage cost? My response was, "Do I have a deal for you." I gave him an excellent price for my fuselage and it turned out that by selling all the bits and pieces, one at a time, we had made more gross profit than for any Champ delivered up to that time. There is more than one way to skin a cat, and thus an aircraft salesman was born.

Before I started to work for Robinson Aviation, I seriously considered flying for one of the major airlines. However, with one exception, I didn't like the attitudes of the airlines about hiring pilots. All airlines I had talked to wanted a minimum of 2,000 hours total time. It didn't matter what kind of flying—fighter pilot, bomber pilot or transport pilot, but you had to have 2,000 hours or they wouldn't talk to you. I had something over 1,800 hours, mostly in Col. Joe Duckworth's high priority Instrument Instructors Training Program. In the Air Force it was second in priority only to the Manhattan (atomic bomb) Project. Col. Joe taught the Air Force how to fly full panel instruments at a time most

Air Force pilots were still flying needle & ball. However, none of this experience mattered to American, United and the others.

The one exception was Pan Am. I almost went with them, because I liked their attitude. When all the other airlines required 2,000 hours, Pan Am required only 500 hours. When I asked why, the answer was, "Anyone we hire will have the potential of becoming the President of Pan Am. We can teach anyone how to fly." I liked that attitude.

At Pan Am I also had one of my most memorable job interviews. It was with the well-known Sam Prior, the number two man after Juan Trippe, the head man of Pan Am during its heyday as the international flag carrier for the United States. He was a good business friend of my father who got me the interview. Sam spent about 45 minutes of his very valuable time trying to talk me out of working in aviation. To help illustrate his point he said, "Al, if I had my present job in your father's company, I would be making twice the money I make here at Pan Am." I said, "If that is true, how come you are here?" I'll never forget his answer, which was, "Well, I guess I just like being around airplanes." This has been the story of my professional life.

Robinson Aviation was a great place to be when the aviation business exploded after WW II. "A plane in every garage" was the thinking at the time. Keith Davis was General Manager and Charlie Parker was the Sales Manager for the fixed base operation part of our company—we also had a shock-mount (manufacturing) division and a small airline called Robinson Airlines. Keith and Charlie were well known for coming up with the idea for circumventing the pre-war Neutrality Act prohibiting flying military aircraft to Canada, England and France. They knew that the airport at Moulton, ME was half in the US and half in Canada. Their solution was to land at Moulton and push the aircraft across the border into Canada. All legal and above-board, because the plane wasn't "flown" into Canada.

Robinson Airlines was kind of neat. Mr. Robinson had a home in Ithaca, NY and owned a Fairchild 24 four-place, single-engine monoplane. On Monday mornings he would fly to Teterboro and on Friday he would fly back to Ithaca. Some friends in Ithaca offered to share expenses if they could ride with him. More than he had room for in his Fairchild. So, he bought a second Fairchild and hired a pilot and began regular service. Soon they were running three Continental powered (more horsepower) twin Beeches. Later, after acquiring three DC-3s from Pan Agra in South America, it became Mohawk Airlines with expanded coverage. Mohawk was acquired by Allegheny Airlines and now, I suppose, is all part of US Air.

There were always interesting people around our facility. One was Leighton Collins, publisher of *Air Facts* magazine and father of *Flying* magazine's Dick Collins. Leighton owned a pre-war Culver Cadet, which he brought to us for service. We were friends until his death a few years back. Another was Boris Sergievski who was a test pilot for Igor Sikorski in his pre-war days. Igor didn't have much money in his early days, so he paid Boris in what later became good United Aircraft stock and made him wealthy by the end of WW II. Boris was also smart enough to marry a wealthy woman. He kept his Grumman Mallard in our hangar. The Mallard (an amphibian) was the fanciest corporate airplane of its day. I often chased down unusual parts for Boris.

Diagonally across Industrial Avenue from us was Atlantic Aviation. Atlantic, at Teterboro, was run by the flamboyant and charismatic Sid Nesbitt. He was the person after whom Zack Moseley patterned his flying character, Smiling Jack, in his comic strip of the same name. Sid was my idol and I thought he was the best airplane salesman there was. Can you imagine, he actually sold those big Twin Beeches and high performance Bonanzas? Incidentally, a Bonanza sold for $6,995 at that time. He also had a demo pilot named Neil Fulton, who I had worked with during my brief career at Atlantic Central Airlines. He later went on to be the Director of Aviation for Olin-Matheson Chemical Corporation.

One day a rather dapper man walked in to our hangar to look over our Culver V demonstrator. The V was a small two-place high performance monoplane, powered with an 85 horsepower, fuel-injected Continental. He handed me his business card showing him to be in the import/export business and the name on the card was Colonel Lance Call. He bought the V and I had to check him out in it. He was an average pilot. Later he brought out his gorgeous secretary (an ex Wasp who later became Mrs. Call) and asked me to check her out also. Believe me, it was my pleasure. She turned out to be a much better pilot than the Colonel.

Years later, after flying C-119s on the Korean Airlift for eleven months, I came home to Sewart AFB near Nashville and discovered that our new Division Commanding General in South Carolina was BG Lance Call. My stock in the Squadron rose considerably when it was learned that I not only knew our new general, but also had actually flown with his well-known, beautiful wife.

Also based with us at Robinson, was the prototype of a very attractive, all wood, four place, twin-engine airplane. The principals were trying hard to promote enough capital to put it into production. One of the principals was often accompanied by his very attractive and well-endowed girl friend. One sunny warm summer day, out on our ramp, they were posing her for publicity pictures up on the wing of their little twin, dressed in white very short shorts and a top that looked like it was made of fish net. She was a sight to behold. The head of our line crew was a good-looking kid in his early twenties. At this point in the proceedings he came out of our hangar carrying a large armload of wheel chocks. He was fascinated by the apparition up on the plane's wing and didn't see a tie-down rope holding one of our Champs. He tripped over it and chocks went flying. Without ever taking his eyes off this luscious creature he picked up all the chocks and continued across the ramp—but never once took his eyes off that gal.

Adak, Alaska

1948 TO 1949

TWO AND A HALF YEARS after starting with Robinson Aviation and getting my feet wet as a budding aircraft salesman, I was invited by my Uncle Sam to come back on active duty with the Air Force. My first assignment was as an Air Installations—Duty Pilot—Base Billeting—Squadron Supply/Mess/and Adjutant Officer on Adak in the Aleutian Islands. Back in the States, any one of these assignments would have been a full-time job. On Adak, I did them all. It really was a fascinating assignment and quite an education. My family and I were there almost two years.

I went to Alaska on the troop ship Funston. On that trip I got the duty of Mess Officer for the trip. Each morning I would go to the Mess Hall to "inspect" the coffee and dessert to make certain they were fit for the troops. Our First Sergeant was usually there also and for the same reason. He was a Master Sergeant and I will call him Bob. We became pretty good friends. A few months later, on one of my frequent cargo runs to Anchorage, I was walking down the hall of the Officers Quarters and I walked by an open door of one of the rooms. Imagine my surprise to see Bob sitting there in civilian clothes. He put out his hand and quickly shut off any questions by telling me that all I needed to know was that he was an FAA inspector. Later, when he showed up on Adak, again

Adak, Alaska. The garden spot of the world.

as a civilian, and I had him out to our house for dinner I learned he was actually a Major in Counter Intelligence working out of the Pentagon. An interesting world.

When I was first at Anchorage, I was told that they were short of Air Installations Officers on every base in the territory. Where would I like to be assigned? I asked what base had the shortest waiting time for dependents to arrive. I was told Adak and I said I'd take it. The personnel man gave me a strange look, like I had lost my mind, and I got the assignment.

My first trip to Adak was interesting. It was on a C-47 from Adak doing its weekly cargo run to Anchorage. We landed at Cold Bay for refueling, the last land on the mainland of Alaska and the beginng of the Aleutian Island Chain. My new boss, Major Marshall, met me as I got off the plane and told me to bring my gear, because I was going to be there several days to assist a civilian crew to drill a well. I told Major Marshall that I knew nothing about drilling wells. His response was that I had a degree in Geology which was more than anyone else in his command had, so therefore I got the job.

As I got my gear off the C47, the Cold Bay Base Commander's wife took my place. She was carrying their very small baby. When I inquired where she was going, I was told she was going to visit her Doctor on Adak (800 miles away) for her six-week check up. This was my first taste of life in the Alaskan Territory. Fortunately for me, the civilian drilling rig crew knew what they were doing and the well came in OK.

Major Jack Marshall was the Base Air Installations Officer and my immediate boss. Jack was a former general contractor and a rough, tough character. He had gotten a broken back in a plane crash during WWII. It left him hunchbacked and with no great enthusiasm for pilots in general. He got me for his Exec Officer. Needless to say, I was not received with great enthusiasm. He completed my Officer Effectiveness Rating about a month after I arrived and I got only an average rating.

About this same time, Jack asked me to look into a problem in our carpentry shop. On Adak we had sudden strong wind-storms (sometimes over 100mph) that we called Williwaws. They could easily blow a door off its hinges. The Carpentry Shop would get a work order request to replace the door and it would take 6 weeks to get new hinges out of Supply. Not a good system. I looked into the situation and recommended a shop stock of commonly used hardware be set up in the Carpentry Shop. The Base Supply Officer stated that it couldn't be done. I looked into the regula-tions and showed Jack just how it *could* be done, and repairs could now be done the same day. Jack now decided that having a pilot around wasn't so bad after all. As it turned out, I became about the only officer Jack could work with.

Among my many other jobs I was the squadron Adjutant and Mess Officer. Our Mess Sergeant was an old hand who had forgot-ten more about running a mess hall than I would ever learn, so I let him run it. I would come in each morning, have a cup of coffee, sample the day's dessert, sign the necessary papers and go on my way. After a few months we got an extra officer, Capt. Baxter—and a West Point Graduate—and he took over my jobs of

Adjutant and Mess Officer. After a few weeks, Jack called me into his office and plaintively asked if I could take back my job as Mess Officer, because the place had become such a shambles. Jack loved to eat. I said certainly and discovered that Baxter had tried to micro-manage everything. As soon as the Mess Hall returned to my hands-off style of management, everything returned to normal. Once again I was a hero in Jack's eyes.

Our Mess Hall not only fed the GI's of the Air Installations Squadron, but all the civilians in our many shops as well. It was reputed to serve the best food on the Chain. We even had Northwest Airlines crews ask to eat with us. We had a Staff Sergeant Sladky who turned out to be a first class baker. When we found out about his skill, we went out to one of the abandoned areas of our base, put a complete bake shop on a large flatbed and added it to our mess hall. Sgt. Sladky got to be a full time baker making special birthday cakes and other goodies for all the people using our mess hall.

Our big boss for Air Installations at Command Headquarters in Anchorage was Colonel Adolph Kroeber. "Dolph" was a very interesting person and one of the finest officers I have known. He had a most interesting background. He had been a Nazi Brown Shirt in the early days of Hitler's regime. In the mid thirties "Dolph" didn't like the direction Hitler was going, so he moved his family to the United States. Here he joined the National Guard. World War Two came along and he ended up a Colonel in the U.S. Air Force. He gave the appearance of the classical Hollywood Prussian officer.

He also was very sharp and an excellent officer to work with. Periodically he made inspection trips to Adak to keep an eye on our Air Installations operations and also, I'm sure, to make certain that our Mess Hall was maintaining its high standards. At the end of the day, after supper, he would often like to play Cribbage and I would usually get challenged. If I began to run up too good a score, I would be gently reminded by "Dolph" that he still had need for an Air Installations Officer on St. Lawrence Island, in the Bering Sea about 60 Miles off the coast of Siberia. It was amazing how quickly my luck would change at that point. We remained good friends until he passed away a few years ago

At the end of WWII, Adak was a 10,000 man base. When I got there in 1948, it was down to about 1,500 military and perhaps 1,000 civilians. Therefore whole areas of the base were simply abandoned. These abandoned buildings were the first line of supplies for the various Air Installations shops. By the time I got there these sources were beginning to dry up and regular sources were in trouble because they had no history of consumption to set stock levels. The result was chaos in the supply system.

By 1949 the brand new Air Force resolved the whole problem by deciding to sell the whole Davis Air Force Base to the Navy. Being the Real Property Officer for the Base, I got the job of packaging up the base and its records and turning it over to the Navy. This idea of selling the base to the Navy was a first for the newly independent Air Force. When I started the project, I was accountable for 4,200 buildings and their installed property—many of which had blown away in Williwaws. I was fortunate to have a mentor in Commander Costello, who was my counterpart on the Navy side of Adak. He took me under his wing and guided me through the maze. To make a long story short, we wrote off, on paper, 4,158 of these war-time shacks and sold the remaining 42 buildings to the Navy. The remaining buildings were the few good buildings such as Base Headquarters, the Chapel, the Theater and the Base Hospital. Martha and I extended our tour on Adak about six months to finish that project and also to return stateside during a nicer time of the year. We returned to the States in May 1950.

Flight to the Far East

AUGUST & SEPTEMBER 1950

ANYONE WHO HAS STUDIED Political Geography will recognize that the Korean War pitted two unrelated geopolitical factors of powerhood against each other. China, and its subsidiary North Korea, had the powerhood factor of Unlimited Manpower on its side, against which the United States successfully pitted its powerhood factor of Technology.

One of the key elements of the US Air Force's use of advanced technology in Korea was its ability to re-supply ground forces by air. We also had total air superiority. For the Chinese and North Koreans to move supplies it was necessary to load everything on A-frames on the backs of men. USAF relied on airlift for re-supply of fast moving armored columns and didn't have to quickly rebuild bridges or rail lines to keep the supplies moving. If a UN unit was cut off, it was easy to air drop supplies to keep them going until they were relieved or they fought their way out. If a unit ran out of something critical, like mortar shells, and notified Combat Cargo in the evening, they would be air-dropped to them at sun up. In an emergency, it could be done in four hours—including 1 1/2 hours of flying time.

The USAF had good experience with high volume Airlift techniques during the well-publicized Berlin Airlift. However, in Korea (the "Forgotten War"), USAF was presented with a much more

Al Conklin—pilot

complicated problem. For example, in Berlin there were only a handful of good airports serviced by three air corridors. The variety of cargo carried was relatively limited. Korea on the other hand had many corridors, dozens of airports—many simply gravel strips—and the cargoes were infinitely variable—artillery shells, woolen socks, ice cream freezers, 6x6 trucks, bridges, rations, open bottles of Nitro-Glycerin and Officers Club supplies, to name a few that I carried. And, for variety, there were the hundreds of aerial re-supply missions.

Little has been written about the Korean Airlift, but it really was a lot more complicated and a much more diverse operation than the Berlin Airlift. This story is about the then brand new C-119 Flying Boxcars, which were the backbone of the diverse capability that permitted the Combat Cargo Command to meet its varied requirements. This chapter, *Flight to the Far East,* tells about the movement of the 314th Troop Carrier Group from Nashville, TN to the Far East "To participate in the activities thereof."

I was recalled to active duty in June 1948 to attend the Air Installation Staff Officers Course at the Air Force Institute of

Technology at Wright-Patterson AFB. In October 1948 I was assigned as an Air Installations Officer to Adak in the Aleutian Islands. There, among many other jobs, I was a duty pilot flying C-47s all over Alaska. In May 1950 my family and I rotated back to the States and ended up at the Troop Carrier base at Sewart AFB in Smyrna, TN, outside Nashville. Sewart was probably the only AF Base, at that time, with a surplus of AIOs. With my instrument training and weather flying background I was assigned to the 61st Troop Carrier Squadron. This is our story.

Sewart was my first assignment to a tactical unit. We were the first group to be given the new C-119 Flying Boxcars. They had not been given the usual Service Testing period before being handed to the tactical units. We, actually, were to provide the Service Testing in our normal operations. An interesting situation, in view of the fact that we were in Korea within 90 days.

In August we were alerted for 60 days Temporary Duty in Japan and Korea. Up to that point I had only flown the Boxcar from the copilot's seat and, generally, while towing 2 Waco gliders to and around Fort Bragg with the Airborne 187th Regimental Combat Team. After we were alerted, our Group was suddenly jumped from 18 to 24 aircraft in each Squadron. Because of my high total time and instrument flying experience, I was suddenly moved to the left seat, given a couple of single-engine procedures, a couple of circuits and bounces by Capt. Moose Johnson and pronounced a C-119 pilot. I was fortunate to have over 3,000 hours of civilian and military flying time, but we suddenly had a couple of new left-seaters who only had about 750 hours total time.

I was assigned to a brand new aircraft, #132, just brought in from Fairchild's plant in Hagerstown, MD. It had about 12 hours total time in its logbook when handed to me. My copilot, Bert Christoffers, was an M-Day Assignee who had been flying C-119s in the Reserves at Sewart. Chris came on active duty three days before we left for Japan. Sgt. Jack Morton, my crew-chief, was a real blessing. We had no formal ground-school, simulators or anything for this new aircraft and Morton taught me everything about its engines and systems. Later I realized that Jack was the best crew chief in the whole group. I learned as we went along. Sgt. Red Mathis was our radio operator and had been with the 449th All Weather Fighter Squadron on Adak about the same time I was there. When he found out there was an experienced Aleutian pilot in the squadron, he figured I couldn't be all-bad, so he wangled his way onto my crew.

So on Friday, three days before departing for the Far East, we all met and got acquainted with each other and our nice new flying machine. Chris was a bachelor and had just moved his gear onto the base. He decided to sell his car and asked if there was anything we might need that he could get with the money from the car. I remembered reading about some of the Berlin Airlift crews carrying motor scooters aboard their C-54s for ground transportation and suggested the idea to Chris. On my way home, Friday night, I passed Chris on the highway heading for Sewart on his new Cushman scooter. It went with us all the way to Japan, providing us with ground transportation wherever we went, but never managed to show up on the loading manifest.

On Monday morning, August 30, 1950, along with Capt. Maurice "Moose" Johnson and Capt. Bill Doyle in our lead aircraft, Lts. Ewert and Martin in the number two aircraft and Chris and I in the number three slot, we fired up, taxied out and took off for Castle AFB in Merced, CA. Keep in mind, I was so green in this fine new aircraft that that Monday morning was the first time I had actually started those wonderful big 28 cylinder Corn-Cob engines all by myself. Jack Morton coached me through the procedure.

Moose, in his preflight briefing, said that we would lock up the formation right after takeoff and buzz the runway because we knew that the wives were all parked off the end of the runway to watch our departure. Great idea! All of our birds were loaded to the gills with extra fuel tanks in the cabin, 6 to 8 passengers back there and all kinds of spare parts plus one motor scooter.

I was #3 to take off and was really eager to look good in the eyes of Moose and Ewert, both veteran C-119 drivers. We took off at seven-second intervals. The procedure was for the lead aircraft to fly the runway heading for two minutes, then make a 180-degree left turn back and the other two aircraft would anticipate the turn and slide into position. Ewert would take Moose's right wing and I would take the left. Well, I was really pushing ol' 132, anxious to get quickly into position so we would look good for the wives on the ground.

Remember that almost all my experience with C-119s up to that point was towing gliders. Well, on that Monday morning I had a clean aircraft, at full gross weight. Everything looked great as I came up on Moose's left wing and I started to ease off the power to slow down. 132 simply had too much momentum and too little drag to want to slow down. I finally had full power off and was still passing Moose. Very embarrassing to look like the lead aircraft when you are supposed to be number three. Finally, as I was looking straight across at Moose, we finally began to slow down, back up and finally slid into the proper position just before we got back to the field. We got a grand wave from the gals and kids as we roared by overhead and headed off to California.

Bert Christoffers—copilot.

Red Mathis—radio operator.

The trip to California went off without a hitch. We went by way of Memphis, Fort Worth (right over Hicks Field where I attended Primary School), El Paso, Tucson, Los Angeles and then north up the San Joaquin Valley to Merced. For the first couple of hours we were on instruments, but by the time we reached Dallas it was CAVU (Ceiling and Visibility Unlimited) and clear all the rest of the way. None of our aircraft missed a beat all the way. A delightful trip.

We flew a very loose formation, all the way, until we were a few miles south of Castle AFB. Then we moved in close, locked it up and flew a tight formation with the wings overlapped by several feet and performed a 360 degree overhead peel-off that even our Sqdn. CO, Major McNulty, would have been proud of. McNulty had flown Spitfires with the Eagle Squadron in England and he was insistent that we fly the Boxcars the same way "they had flown their Spitfires." Even the guys on the ground commented on the good looks of our formation, but we just gave them the old Magoo about how we just fly them that way all the time. Our flying time to California was just about 12 hours.

Tuesday morning we were up at 0400 for our briefing for the flight to Hawaii at 0500. Then we made out our clearances and went out to check our aircraft. I was angry that they had just shifted our plane to the flight ahead of Moose's. However, as we checked over 132 we discovered a minor gas leak that delayed us just long enough to put us back into my original flight. However, all my finagling was to no avail. Just as our flight was taxiing out, the lead ship in the flight ahead of us had engine trouble and had to abort. Moose was instructed to take that lead and Ewert and I were assigned to another flight. When we finally got airborne Ewert had to abort because of flap trouble and I found myself a lonesome 61st Squadron man on some stranger's wing.

The weather was beautiful, sunny and warm. Ahead and slightly below was the lead aircraft. We flew in three ship formations with a navigator in the lead aircraft. On board everyone happily settled down for the long grind ahead. In the back of the cabin was a small poker game. 3 or 4 of our passengers made themselves comfortable on top of the luggage and were either resting or reading. Up in the front office Mathis monitored his radio equipment, Morton kept his eyes on the engine instruments, Chris kept all the logs and filled out the paperwork, while George, our autopilot, did the flying.

A few hours out we passed over Nan, the radio navigational fix on a ship near the mid-point to Hawaii. I got out my chart and, with my fingers spread out, measured off the distance to Hickham, did some quick mental arithmetic and estimated our total flight time to our destination as fourteen hours from our original take-off time. A little while later the navigator in our lead ship gave us an estimate of twelve hours. This startled me, but I figured he had celestial and Loran equipment and was a rated navigator so, what did I know? Well, twelve hours came and went, as did thirteen and fourteen hours. We landed at Hickham fourteen hours and twenty minutes after our takeoff. This was not a confidence builder to have to follow this navigator the rest of the way across the Pacific. I later found out that he too had just been recalled to active duty and this was the first time he had been in an aircraft since WW II! How lucky could we get?

We landed a little before dark, got a bite to eat and were airborne by 0300 Hawaii Time. Eight hours was the maximum time permitted for refueling and rest. As we parked our plane, Blanton and Gause met us all decked out in fancy flowered Aloha shirts. When they had taken off, two days before, one of their engines caught fire and they made an emergency single-engine landing. While they were waiting for an engine change, they were having a fine visit in Honolulu with a big room at the Royal Hawaiian complete with "whiskey and wild, wild women." They were obviously enjoying their misfortune and didn't hesitate to let us know how sorry they were that they would be delayed getting to "our shooting war."

Wednesday, 1 September, found us on our way to Johnson Island about 522 miles SW of Hickham. An interesting piece of geology. They actually enlarged the island to get the necessary length (5700 feet) for the runway. Most of the island is not much wider than the runway itself and the elevation is only seven feet. There isn't a tree or a clump of grass on this little atoll. Almost no atoll at all.

Our stop on Johnson was only long enough to refuel, make out clearances and have a bite to eat. Johnson and Doyle were on the island when we landed and running about 35 to 45 minutes ahead of us. Then it was off to Kwajalein Atoll, in the Marshall Islands, 1222 miles west of Johnson.

A most interesting leg on our trip. If measured on a calendar the trip lasted 32 hours. This resulted from our crossing the International Dateline in the afternoon and jumped from Friday afternoon directly into Saturday afternoon. We also flew about four hours of thick weather through the Inter-Tropical Front. Back at Sewart I was shown once, on a blackboard, something called a Troop Carrier Weather Penetration. In it the lead aircraft flies straight ahead, the number two aircraft turns right 45 degrees for one minute, climbs 500 feet and resumes course, while number

Jack Morton—crew chief.

three turns left 45 degrees for one minute, descends 500 feet and resumes the original heading. On the blackboard this all looked pretty neat, but as we approached this real Front I began to wonder about all this. It looked great on paper, but would it really work?

We executed the Penetration exercise and I saw the other two aircraft disappear into the frontal weather and we were on solid instruments for over four hours. I really worried about how I was ever going to find Kwajalein, especially with sunset approaching. Guess what? Even after the navigator, in the lead plane, gave us several 3 and 4 degree heading changes, we broke out in the clear on the south side of that front and there were both of the other planes essentially where I'd seen them when we entered that big front. Wow! Was I ever surprised and relieved. It worked like a charm.

As we approached Kwaj it rapidly turned dark and began to rain very hard and we had to make an instrument approach. I had only landed the C-119 a couple of times at night and the weather had been great. To add to my unhappy state of mind, as we turned on final for landing the hollow glass windshield steamed up inside from the high humidity and the defrost couldn't get rid of it. The ship ahead of me executed a go around and I didn't want to try to follow him around with no forward visibility. I could barely make out the glow of the Bartow lights, so continued my approach. In my fumbling around and feeling for the runway I somehow managed to grease it on exactly like I knew what I was doing. My crew and passengers thought I was pretty hot. If they had known how unhappy I had felt or how lucky that landing was they would have, no doubt, had a much lower opinion of their driver, but from that point on I really had the confidence of my crew. This is another example of my Instructor Pilot's help.

A large portion of the 61st Squadron was there when we parked our aircraft. Johnson and Doyle, of course, and Tarbox, Teare, Buckley and Moore who had all had minor maintenance problems or were just plain bushed and had laid over a day. Most of our gang were all billeted in a big Quonset hut. That front keeps Kwaj in and out of rain showers all the time during that time of the year. Sure enough, in the middle of the night the roof sprang a leak right over my bed.

In the morning we all took off in our respective flights during heavy rain showers and were soon winging our way to Guam for our last stay-over of the trip. It was an uneventful leg. We still didn't know our ultimate destination. All we knew was "to the Far East Air Force to participate in activities thereof." The quaint language of our orders.

We landed Sunday at Anderson AFB, where they told us that we probably would not be able to get off until Tuesday because of refueling problems and also because of a small typhoon between Guam and Japan. So, Monday we all slept late for the first time since starting this little trip. In the middle of the afternoon we hopped over to NOB Agana, about 15 miles away, to refuel. In departing for Agana I latched onto Moose Johnson's flight. It was so late in the day that we stayed there overnight.

Just prior to departing Anderson for Agana to refuel, Col. Henderson (our Group CO) and his flight landed—including

Ewert and Martin who we hadn't seen since they turned back in California. Col. Henderson had a nose wheel shimmy damper let go on his landing roll and blew out three tires trying to keep his ship under control and getting it stopped. He almost clobbered the plane in the process. Some excitement!

The Colonel also told us about hearing that we'd lost another ship back at Sewart with seven killed and three getting out. It obviously was one of our group and we were anxious to get more details. This whole trip seemed to have been dogged by trouble the whole way. Our plane #132, however, just kept purring like a kitten the whole way, so we had no complaints on that score.

Our one night at Anderson found us billeted in a hut out in the sticks. As a matter of fact, we were about 50 yards from the hut Christoffers lived in when he was stationed there in '46 and '47. However, at Agana the Navy treated us to their usual courtesy and comforts. The main points being: billeted right next to the nurses quarters, excellent food served at tables with table cloths (no cafeteria style for the Navy) and an excellent club with drinks so cheap one could hardly afford to stay sober. Being back with Johnson and Doyle also made for good company.

On 5 September we reluctantly departed Guam and headed for Japan by way of Iwo Jima. Looking ahead about 10 miles I thought I could see Mt. Suribachi on Iwo. However, Doyle quickly advised me that it really was Amami O Shima (or some such name) and that Iwo was about 35 miles further down the road. Iwo looked like any of the small islands in the Aleutians. It was a desolate looking place, real flat except for Mt. Suribachi and was shaped like a baked Virginia ham. There were a couple of runways and a few buildings scattered around. Our next landfall would be Japan. We were slowly getting there. It would be good to see some real terra firma. This had been one long haul.

Buckley's flight—the one just ahead of us—just got the word, via radio, that their destination, which was the same as ours, had been changed. And we stood by to see if ours would be changed also. As usual the confusion was highly organized. Yes, our destination was changed also. We were now on our way to Komaki Air Base just outside Nagoya. Nagoya was one of the four or five largest cities in Japan and home of Mitsubishi Industries. A nice location on the east-side of the island of Honshu and about 160 miles SW of Tokyo. Up ahead we could see Fujiyama, the most famous mountain in Japan. Fuji is most impressive, but no more so than Shisholdin or Pavlov on the Aleutian chain.

Well, here we are on the 6th of September, at long last, at Komaki AB, Nagoya, Japan. Eight days from the time I was alerted, until I arrived at Komaki. Not a bad average. We didn't have a single write-up for maintenance on the entire trip until we were in the traffic pattern at Komaki. When we extended the landing gear, the left main gear remained retracted and we had to hand crank it down. Practically nothing, and probably no other aircraft did that well on the trip.

Komaki is very nice, but somewhat small. The terrain and climate are much like southern California—very warm, level ground and with fairly rugged mountains in the distance. We were the only outfit on the base, but, even so, we were put up in big 15' x 30' ten-man tents. While not very lush in accommodations, we were, as a result of the climate, very comfortable. The big draw-back to the base was that everything was in town—movies, PX, Post Office, supply warehouse and even the Officers Club—which made things difficult. All work on the base, such as construction, KPs, table waiters, clean up details and even fire protection, was performed by "indigenous" personnel. The Japanese are all very hard working people and put most Americans to shame by their hard work.

By Japanese standards, Nagoya was a pretty nice city. It was still in bad shape from the fire bombing raids of WW II. Most buildings in Japan were constructed out of wood and all were destroyed during the war. The rebuilding process was just getting started. Only a few modern reinforced concrete buildings were left standing in the heart of the city. What came as a surprise to me was to find the Japanese were very friendly to Americans. They did a land office business with the GIs who were buying such things as bicycles—the chief means of transportation in post war Japan—to sets of fancy dinnerware.

Taxicabs were of two types. The more common being a three-wheeled motorcycle, a little like a short open touring car, and the other being a small electric sedan, a little like a small Austin, only much narrower. Only two very round-shouldered Americans could sit in the back without overlapping. There were very few cars or trucks because of the lack of gasoline. What few we saw were converted to burning charcoal. These big, dirty and smoking charcoal burners were built onto the back end of the vehicle and smell and smoke up the whole town.

Our stay at Komaki was to be short lived. On the 9th of September we were off to Ashiya on Kyushu, directly across the Sea of Japan from Pusan, Korea. This turned out to be our final destination for our stay in Japan. The 61st squadron moved that day and were the first to move into our new home.

Ashiya was a delightful, modest sized base right on the Sea of Japan. During WW II it had been a training base for Kamikaze pilots who were obviously well treated. It is larger than Komaki and was complete with theater, PX and even a few families. We didn't have to ride into town every time we wanted something.

They put 12 of us officers in a very nice set of family quarters—four to a bedroom, a kitchenette, living room and a good-sized bathroom. There were also two Mamasans who did all the house-keeping chores and laundry. We were located about 100 yards from the Officer's Mess, Officers Club, Theater and PX— all pretty convenient. Originally I was supposed to room with Doyle, Johnson and Heft, but Major McNulty, in his infinite wisdom, decided that the Captains would all be in one house and the 1st Lts. would be in another. Christoffers, Knie and Martin became my roommates.

On the 10th we became "combat veterans" when we all took familiarization rides in Gooney Birds (C-47) over to Korea. Don't laugh. It really counted as a combat mission on our records. Also in the plane I was in were Johnson and Buckley. We carried in high priority supplies and carried out wounded GIs. The single runway at Pusan was pierced steel plank and there was a veritable beehive of activity. Single C-47s were continually landing and taking off on missions similar to ours. About every 15 minutes a flight of four P-51 Mustangs took off for the front which was anywhere from 15 to 45 miles away. They were loaded down with four large rockets and two 1,000 lb. bombs slung under their wings. Only the P-51 fighters could routinely operate out of the few fields that were left in South Korea at that time. The jets all operated out of Japan. And of course the little liaison planes and helicopters were buzzing in and out all the time. Korean laborers were all over the place repairing the pierced steel mating or loading and unloading the C-47s. So we got our introduction to flying in Korea.

The Korean Airlift

SEPTEMBER 1950 TO JUNE 1951

Combat Cargo Command

 THE FAIRCHILD C-82 PROVED THE CONCEPT of putting a wing and engines on a boxcar for use as a cargo airplane. However, it was underpowered. Fairchild went back to the drawing board and proposed the C-119, a greatly improved model. It went right from the drawing board into production and, without the usual service testing, went right on active duty with the 314th TC Group. It was powered by two Pratt & Whitney R4360 "Corncob" twenty eight cylinder radial engines that, with water injection, produced 3500 horsepower for takeoff. It was slightly larger than the C-82, was the AF first all electric (110 volt) aircraft and could outdo, on two engines, the C-54 with its four engines. It was easy to fly in formation and very stable on instruments. Although it needed a fair amount of debugging, it was a great airplane to fly.

Its shortcomings were a structure not meant to take the continual beating of operating out of short, gravel airstrips. Although we did it, the C-119 was not intended to be operated out of small, unimproved runways. It also was not a good performer with one engine out. All of us recommended four engines for the next cargo plane, which became the Lockheed C-130, designed to incorporate all the things we learned in Korea.

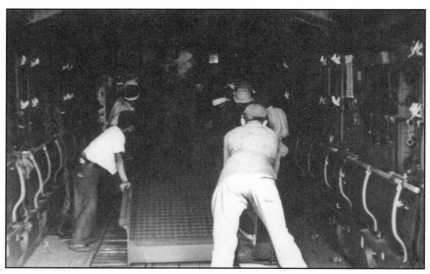

Loading a section of Treadway Bridge the day before General
MacArthur used it to cross the Han River into Seoul.

Despite its weaknesses, the C-119s of the 314th TCG gave the
Combat Cargo Command its much-needed versatility. The other
organizations, with their C-54s, C-47s, C-46s and the Royal
Canadian Air Force C-54M (Merlin powered C-54), could all
carry cargo. However, only the Boxcars could air drop tons of supplies in one pass or drop heavy equipment, such as a 6x6 truck, or
the sections of a Bailey Bridge. And, of course, they were much
better adapted to dropping airborne troops.

Our group of C-119s arrived at Ashiya, Japan on September
9, 1950. For the next week we spent our time getting briefed on
Air-Sea Rescue and also on Escape and Evasion techniques. Other
time was spent on our local swimming beach about 100 yards off
the end of our runway. And, of course, we got our aircraft ready
for the big push we knew would be coming soon. At this time we
still didn't know just why the big rush to get our aircraft to the Far
East, but with many members of the 187th Airborne Regimental
Combat Team at Ashiya, we thought we could guess.

On the 14th of September it started to really rain. We were
advised that a typhoon was a couple of hundred miles south of us

and to report to our Operations. By the time we got there the "Panic Button" had been pushed and the place was a madhouse. The only field that was open in Japan was Haneda, just outside Tokyo. They wanted us to use Ashiya as an alternate, but it was already at minimums and deteriorating. They did get three aircraft off before Ashiya went below minimums and then they called off the mission.

Later, someone at Group got the bright idea of having those of us with Green Instrument Cards (there were only seven in the whole group) sign our clearances and go. By this time the wind was gusting to 45 Knots and 90 degrees across the runway and pouring down rain. I proposed that we use a technique we had used to protect our C-47s from Williwaws (sudden high winds) up in the Aleutians. Get a crew in each airplane and literally fly the plane, on the ground, nose into the wind, until the storm was over. Safe, inexpensive and worked like a charm.

The seven of us with green cards agreed that we would not sign our own clearances, because of the poor weather, no alternate airport and our unfamiliarity with the destination. However, if given a direct order by Gen. Tunner (newly in place and organizing the chaos of early Airlift) and he signed the clearance, then we would go. Shortly Group canceled the mission. We spent the night in our planes, kept them pointed into the wind and had no trouble at all. We felt justified in our stand after we learned that one crew from the 62nd Squadron did take off and was blown into a close-by mountain, destroying one $550,000 airplane and killing four crewmen.

On the 16th, the Marines landed at Inchon, a few miles west of Seoul. Our Group Commander told us that within a very few days we would be flying around the clock. On 18 September our ship (#132) and my crew—Bert Christoffers (copilot), Jack Morton (crew chief) and "Red" Mathis (radio operator) were the first C-119 from our squadron to fly into Korea.

The briefing for this trip was most interesting. Weather was IFR (instruments) all the way to our destination at Taegu (K-2). The Group Operations Officer told us "to fly instruments to the

Pusan range station on the east coast of Korea, make a let down over the Sea of Japan and, if we broke out, we were to fly back VFR (Visual Flight Rules) to Pusan. If not, then we were to return IFR to Ashiya. After reaching Pusan we were to keep to the left of the city and pick up the Naktong River and follow it to the second fork in the river. It would be easy to recognize, because there was a railroad bridge at that point. Follow the railroad to the right and it will take you to Taegu, your destination. Be careful following the railroad up that valley if the overcast is down on top of the hills. Where the valley narrows, be especially careful. If you can't see through that narrow section, don't enter it, because the valley will be too narrow to turn around in. If you can see through, you will be OK and Taegu will be on the other side."

I asked him what altitude I should fly at and was told to pick an altitude. When I asked him what altitude the P-51s were flying at or the B-26s he didn't know. "Just pick an altitude." I said no thanks, that I'd fly VFR underneath. He looked at me like I was crazy, but we went across the Sea of Japan on the deck where it was "safe." At 500 feet it was very rainy and we were in and out of it, but with a Radio Altimeter we flew instruments through the showers at 500 feet and hit Pusan right on the nose. The rest of the trip was as briefed. Not fancy, but it worked and we didn't chew off some ones tail in the overcast.

Taegu was a fighter strip surfaced with PSP (Pierced Steel Planking). It was located just inside of the perimeter we held in South Korea. There were US and Australian P-51s all over the place. We ate lunch, C rations, at the Officers Mess—a twenty foot square room at one end of a building near the Flight Line. I was not able to imagine myself sitting in the Officers Mess at Randolph Field or the Navy Mess at Agana a few days before. Alongside one of the small hangars on the field I saw a little wrecked Stinson Station Wagon. It brought back memories of the good times selling them at Teterboro a few years earlier. It sure looked out of place among all the fighters. After lunch we returned to Ashiya without further adventures.

On the 17th, about 9:30 PM, the Marines took Kimpo Airport, about three miles outside Seoul. On the 18th, Dick Knie and some others flew in all the radio, personnel, weather and other equipment needed to make Kimpo operational. That night, just as Dick was taxiing out for takeoff, the north Koreans laid down a mortar barrage on the airport. Dick needed no help getting off. He claimed he was airborne in 75 feet.

The Korean Airlift really began the next day—the 19th of September. It was really organized. In the few days that General Tunner had been in the Far East, he and his staff really did a super job of organizing the air operations throughout Korea. Gone forever was the chaos of earlier operations. They laid out a corridor starting at Fukuoka—a few miles southwest of our base at Ashiya—going west along the south coast of the Korean Peninsula, then north, just off the west coast, to Inchon and then east to Kimpo. The long way around, but it kept us from flying over 140 miles of enemy-held territory between Taegu and Seoul. We were all assigned altitudes and departed at precise takeoff times. We all knew the tail numbers of several ships ahead of and behind us and this permitted us to maintain our position.

There were a couple of homing stations on ships along the route and we all made position reports as we passed overhead. This made it easy to track our relative position in the traffic stream. We all flew at the slower speed of the C-54s and we were given little charts with power changes needed to speed up or slow down to correct our interval. Everything was well organized and a great relief from the airway anarchy of just a few days before.

I am a big enthusiast for General Tunner. He is a great organizer. In the months ahead I saw him all over the place and at all times of the day or night. He was a hands-on person. I'd be helping with the unloading of my aircraft and a Jeep would roll up with a driver and the General in fatigues and no obvious insignia of rank. He would ask how things were going. If all was OK he would move on. If there was a problem, he wanted to know about it and what we would suggest to correct it. The suggestion was usually in place within the next day or so. He actually listened to his troops. One awful night three months later, during the evacuation of the Marines at Hamhung, one of the Colonels in our group was trying to pull his rank to get a load and was really messing things up. At this point Gen. Tunner walked in. He listened for a bit, then ordered the Colonel to get into his aircraft, return to Ashiya and not return to Korea again. The Colonel was soon on his way back to the states. General Tunner was my kind of "no nonsense" guy.

Sgt. Morton and Sgt. Blankenship (our ground crewchief) with our #1 Japanese helper. Sugi Kept our plane clean and painted our "trash can" mission symbols on 132's nose.

On that first day, our trip was quite uneventful. We were on instruments the first two of our three-hour flight around the peninsula. As we neared Inchon, where the Marines had landed, we could see the feverish activity of the ships. Several fires in the port area were still to be seen. Even the "Big Mo" (battleship Missouri) was there.

Kimpo was about 5 miles northeast of Inchon and just that morning the Marines had crossed the Han River about 1 1/2 miles NE of Kimpo. We knew that the Marines were making good time, but just to play safe we asked for a straight-in approach on the NE runway.

Our friends in the Navy had not been kind to us. In working over Kimpo the day before, they had succeeded in planting a couple of large bombs on the main runway. This left us with the short (3,500 foot) NE/SW runway. This was interesting, because we had

The pin up girl on the nose of our 132.

been told back at Sewart that the C-119 would never be operated from runways shorter than 6,000 feet. Aside from the main runway at Kimpo, which later became operational, I don't recall ever seeing a 6,000 foot runway during our Airlift operations in Korea. But with good multiple disc brakes and reversing props we did OK.

Kimpo was a wreck. It formerly had been the destination of Northwest Airlines. The buildings were all shot up and burned out. Scattered around the field were the hulks of several Russian-built Yak fighters, light bombers and one Stinson 165. Strangely enough when we went into the shell of the one large hangar we found hidden under a lot of debris two unscratched Yak light single-engine bombers. They had been hidden there by the North Koreans during the day and rolled out at night for nuisance raids on the Pusan Perimeter. The Marines took Kimpo so fast that the North Koreans never got a chance to destroy them.

A little later, while helping with the unloading of our plane, General Tunner came over and talked to me for about five minutes about our flight. He was most pleasant and even apologized about the delay in getting us unloaded. We were only on the ground for about 45 minutes.

We fired up, taxied out and took off. Again, we had to use the short NE runway that headed right for the Han River. I'll bet that my takeoff was the first time those Gyrenes ever saw a C-119 simulate a fighter as I did a tight screaming chandelle to the left off the end of the runway. The only item of interest coming back was that we brought back, Bob Miller of the United Press. He had been up with the Marines that morning and wanted to get back to Japan to file his story. We had quite a talk going back. He figured that the war would be over by 20 October, providing Russia and China kept out.

On the 27th we got a rush call to fly the parts of a prefabricated bridge to Kimpo. The Marines had a big offensive going on near Seoul and needed to bridge the Han River right away. Also General MacArthur wanted to enter Seoul in style. We flew the parts to them that night in our C-119s. The trip was uneventful, with the weather "hot and dusty" all the way. We delivered the bridge to them at 0130 in the morning. It was a clear moonlit night and a real pleasure to fly. We left on such short notice that I was the only one aboard from our regular crew. We got back to Ashiya about 0530 and I hit the sack for my first sleep in 48 hours.

And so it went through the first week of October. On the 6th of October we finally got a day off and Christoffers and I went into Kokura to find a sign painter to paint names on our aircraft and to do some window-shopping. The Japanese are a most industrious people especially doing anything with their hands, such as wood carving or sewing. The prices for everything are ridiculously low. For example, a 92 piece set of their best china only cost $45 to $50.

On 8 October we got a "milk run" to Kimpo delivering a load of artillery shells. We even got a 0900 (bankers hours) takeoff. We thought we might have to make a second trip but were a little late getting back so missed having to do a double-header. Chris and I headed for our quarters and got all cleaned up, figured we'd loaf around and make like a vacation. Our dream didn't last long. Just before dinner we got a call to report to Operations and found we had a trip to Itazuki (a ten-minute hop), south, over the hills. Chris couldn't go, so Lt. Muller went as copilot.

After grabbing a bite to eat and rounding up a crew we got over there about 2130. Things were pretty messed up when we got there, so we decided to sleep in our plane. A fringe benefit with the Boxcar is that they are pretty comfortable to sleep in. About 0300 they brought our load out to us. I like to have died when I saw it. It was a large, aircraft refueling trailer. It was so big that we had to remove the wheels to get the beast through the big clamshell doors at the back of the fuselage. You haven't lived until you try to manhandle and winch a refueling trailer, without wheels, into a cargo airplane. It took us 4 1/2 hours to get that thing aboard.

At 0930 we were ready to take off for Kimpo. However, the weather had turned sour and we sat on the end of the runway for over two hours waiting for a clearance. We eventually got back to Ashiya about 1830 that night The plane and crew, except for the

This nose art is self explanatory.

short break in the afternoon and a four hour nap at night, had been on the go for 34 hours. We felt like we had earned our pay.

The operation of Kimpo was an amazing sight to behold. We normally only used the main (6,000 foot) runway. On that one runway a C-54 or C-119 lands every five minutes (the Airlift by Combat Cargo Command). In between those landings would be handled all the Marine fighters stationed at Kimpo, the T-6s used by the Forward Air Controllers, F-51s of the 5th Air Force, F-51s from the Australian Air Force, Helicopters, L-5 Liaison aircraft and the many other smaller UN transports (mostly C-47s).

What really made all this interesting is that we would all land in one direction and then later take off in the opposite direction. The ability of the Marine tower operators to control all this mess was absolutely unbelievable. One afternoon I was on a close base leg, about to turn onto final approach, when the tower operator cleared a flight of four F-51s to take off right at me. I looked at the distance I had to go before touchdown and figured I had it pretty well made. I rolled out on final and dropped my landing flaps and dad-gummed if the tower didn't clear two Marine Corsairs for takeoff. They racked over into a smart left-hand turn as soon as their wheels left the ground and cleared the runway just as I rounded out for my touchdown. What an eye those guys had, as well as a great sense of humor. They never got riled or excited and never goofed it up. Often close, but never dangerous. And they did keep things moving.

On Friday the 13th, Dick Knie led a three-ship formation up to the Port of Wonsan. The South Koreans had been pushing madly up the East Coast of Korea and taken Wonsan about 90 miles north of the 38th Parallel. It is one of the best harbors in Korea and had an old Japanese fighter strip running perpendicular across the peninsula on the south side of the harbor. It had been deserted since the end of WW II. We carried supplies and equipment to help our guys start housekeeping.

There was only one runway, very short, that ran from water's edge to water's edge right across the peninsula, leaving no margin for error. The runway was paved with asphalt, but had lots of weeds growing up through it. It had also accumulated, over the years, a significant layer of salt deposited by the ocean air. As a landing field for a C-119 it left a lot to be desired.

Dick, being the flight leader, was the first to land. He touched down right at the beginning of the runway, got the nose wheel down and threw it into full reverse. Unfortunately, only his right propeller reversed and his bird rotated exactly 90 degrees on the runway, but because of the slick runway surface his plane slid sideways straight down the center of the runway. He quickly got his prop out of reverse, straightened himself out and taxied off the end of the runway without further trouble.

I was number two to land and saw all of Dick's gyrations while I was on downwind. Not a real morale builder for me. I got to thinking about that short, slick runway and trying to figure out the best way to get my props into reverse fast. In my fast checkout back at Sewart, I had been told that the squat switch for the reversers was on the nose-wheel. So my plan was to touch down short and as soon as the main wheels were on the runway, I'd put the throttles into full reverse and when the nose wheel touched down I'd get instant reverse. Sharp thinking, except for one item. The Squat Switch was on the main gear, not the nose gear.

All went according to plan—slow speed, nose very high, main gear right on the end of the runway and then full reverse. The props reversed with our nose several feet in the air. Our nose came crashing down and I thought the nose-wheel was going to come right up through the cockpit floor. At least we stopped short. For many weeks I was known as "Nose-Wheel" Conklin. All I can say is, that after those two landings and no damage to either plane, Fairchild sure knew how to build strong landing gears.

On the 17th of October, the last two of our aircraft from Sewart finally caught up with us. One was flown by Capt. Flanagan (Squadron Maintenance Officer), and the other by Lt. Aldrich. They took six weeks, while we took eight days. They had been dogged by maintenance trouble all the way from Nashville.

We all were on a three-day "stand-down." No flying for the C-119s. Just maintenance. It was quite obvious we were getting ready for a big show north of the 38th Parallel involving the 187th Airborne Regimental Combat Team.

On the 18th the whole 314th TCG moved to Kimpo to pick up the 187th ARCT and get organized. We were to drop our airborne friends from Camp Campbell near the little North Korean town of Sukchon about 30 miles north of the North Korean capitol of Pyongyang. We landed at Kimpo in the morning, marshaling our planes for proper takeoff sequence, loading the parabundles and heavy equipment to be dropped and getting all the last minute details finished up in preparation for the troop drop early the next morning.

Kimpo may have looked busy during the Airlift operations, but that was nothing compared to Kimpo getting ready for the troop drop. On the field were about 85 C-119s, 60 C-47s and a few F-80s and F-51s just in case they were needed. Again we were living aboard our plane and when I looked out of the cockpit window I could see two Australian F-51s parked almost under our right wing. It rained almost continually and anyplace off the taxiway where we were parked was deep mud.

We finally got the last of the parabundles aboard and the monorail (by which we drop the bundles) hooked up about 2100. We hung up our clothes to dry as best they could, unrolled our sleeping bags and hit the sack. I had been flying until about 0130 the morning before, so was really sleepy. All went well for about one hour, when the Airborne guys came back, turned on the lights and rearranged some of the bundles. After about an hour and a half, we were able to get back to sleep again.

At 0430 our paratroopers showed up to get their chutes ready and this time we decided we might as well stay up. It was about this time that we got the word that our takeoff had been delayed and so we sat around waiting for the weather to break. And so it went...

We eventually got off and the drop went without a hitch. The only damage to any of our planes was caused by a 6x6 truck backing into one of our landing gear doors. This was also the first time heavy equipment was dropped in combat. We dropped Jeeps, trailers, anti-tank guns and even some 6x6 trucks. The only equipment damage from the drop was a couple of broken truck springs, but the trucks were usable. The 187th took the town in about 15 minutes after landing on the DZ.

We carried a Life photographer on our aircraft and we ended up with good press coverage in Life later on. This guy even jumped with our troopers. As we departed the Drop Zone, I looked up and saw SCAP, General MacArthur's new Constellation, circling around a couple of thousand feet above our heads with "The Great White Father" himself keeping an eye on things.

On the night of 26 October, an amusing story occurred about one of the Kimpo tower operators. We had all been uneasy about the thought that the Chinese would enter the war. Also there were occasional nuisance raids on Kimpo by small single-engine North Korean airplanes sneaking down at night and dropping small bombs (probably Trench Mortar shells) to keep us all on our toes and a little jumpy.

With this as background, you can appreciate how the boys felt when the Marine night fighters issued a red alert and reported three unidentified bogies approaching Kimpo. There was a mild pushing of the "Panic Button" that left C-119s, C-54s and other assorted aircraft stacked up over Kimpo while the troops on the deck closed up shop.

About this point, one of the C-119 jocks called the tower to advise them that their runway lights were still on. The tower acknowledged and said they would get them turned off. A few minutes later, the same C-119 was again back over the field and the lights were still on. The C-119 driver once again called the tower and told him that "if he didn't want to get his damned head blown off, he'd better get those damned lights off." The tower operator came right back, in a highly agitated sounding voice saying, "Yeah, yeah, I know, but someone stole my Very Pistol (for shooting off signal flares) and that's the only means I have of sounding the alert." War is hell! Fortunately the alarm was a false one.

On the second of November, we had a little different kind of an airdrop mission. This time we dropped big rolls of 6 inch Manila Hawser to the Navy on a beach way up on the East Coast of North Korea. It was a beautiful clear day and the air was as smooth as glass. Our Squadron CO, Major McNulty, led the formation of three ships with Major Gilmore (Exec Officer) as his copilot. Captain Hill (a Flight Commander) and Captain Brindle (Squadron Operations Officer) in the #2 position. How I got into this elite group I don't know, but with a plain old copilot we flew in the #3 slot.

It was a very routine flight and we each dropped, in trail, our rolls of hawser right on target. The only unusual item was that one of Hill's bundles hit a little Korean hut with a thatched roof. The thatched roof literally exploded like it had been hit by a bomb. Very spectacular! Fortunately no one was inside. After we had accomplished our mission, we formed up our three-plane formation and headed back to Ashiya. The air could not have been smoother and flying the C-119s could not have been easier.

As I have said before, McNulty insisted that we fly the C-119s in close formation just like, "he flew Spitfires when he was in the Eagle Squadron" in England. Because you couldn't really see the wing-men from the cockpit of the lead aircraft, it was his custom to come back to the two airborne jumper doors at the aft end of the cabin to check on the position of his wing-men for his normal formation critique after landing.

Shortly after we formed up, I noticed that Hill not only had his wing overlapped with McNulty, but his wing tip was close enough to the right-hand jumper door that the Major could have reached out and changed Hill's LH Nav light. This looked like a neat idea to me, so I matched Hill's position on the Major's left side. Sure enough, in a few minutes McNulty came back, opened the two jumper doors and found two nav lights staring him in the face. He almost died. That's the way we went across Ashiya prior to peeling off for our usual 360 degree overhead fighter style landing approach. Incidentally, 360 degree overhead approaches were illegal for the 5th AF fighters. However the 314th TCG was there on TDY and we just ignored the rule to the anger of the fighter pilots, who claimed we were flying the crates their aircraft were shipped in.

Well, our tight formation must have unnerved McNulty, because when he peeled-off for landing, he overshot the runway and had to go around. Hill and I both landed without too much effort. As the Major came around the second time, Major Gilmore (copilot) called the tower and said, "We're trying it again." Hill and I were parked on our squadron ramp when McNulty taxied in and were standing at attention, as expected, by the nose of our aircraft for the usual post formation critique. He stomped by without a word or a glance in our direction. No critique of our formation flying after that flight or, for that matter, ever again.

China Enters the War

NOVEMBER 1950

ON THE 3RD OF NOVEMBER it was pretty clear that the Chinese had decided to jump in on the side of the North Koreans. For 36 hours they had been pretty well mauling the UN troops up near the Yalu River. On that same day our Squadron Operations got the go-ahead to start working up the crew lists and other pertinent data for our return to the States. Just as Capt. Brindle (Squadron Operations Officer) and the others got well into it, the word came down to forget it. No doubt related to the activities of the Chinese, but tough on morale.

On the 12th of November I started one of my more memorable adventures on the Airlift. We flew in 36 drums of Avgas to a small gravel airstrip near Sinanju, way up on the western side of North Korea just south of the Yalu River that separates North Korea from Manchuria. It was the furthest north airfield in Korea and a little too close to the Chinese Reds to suit me, even though at that point things seemed to be pretty much under control.

It was a most uneventful flight, with beautiful weather all the way, until we made our landing. The gravel strip was quite short and only about 300 feet wide. I touched down right at the end of the dirt runway and let the nose-wheel down. We rolled about 2,000 feet when the nose-wheel tire blew out and the tire shredded. As the shredded tire whipped around it tore out the hydraulic

The pierced steel plank parking area for the 61st Squadron at Ashiya, Japan.

steering lines to the nose-wheel, which cocked sideways and collapsed. We came to an ignoble stop on our nose. As we were sliding to a stop, Sgt. Mathis (Radio Operator and my only regular crew member with me on that trip) unfastened his seat belt, stood up on his chair, released the overhead escape hatch, was out the hatch and standing on the aircraft's nose in front of the copilot's windshield. As the plane came to a stop, he dropped to the ground.

Later, when I questioned him about this feat of speed and coordination, he said, "The first time I ever got into one of these beasts I figured out the best way to get out. And all I could think about was those 36 drums of Avgas behind us in the cabin, all piled up against the front bulkhead." I had never seen him move fast before, but he sure did that day. We all got out OK, with the only wound being to the seat of Mathis' pants as he went out through the escape hatch.

We quickly got two 6x6 trucks and dragged poor ol' 137 backwards off to the left side of the runway. The four of us stood there looking at this sorry sight, when over strolled a rather scruffy looking Staff Sergeant who walked around the nose, came over to me and said, "No sweat, Lieutenant. I can fix it." It turned out that he had been a B-24 Crew Chief in Italy during WW II. They had had a similar problem with one of their B-24s and figured we could fix our aircraft the same way he had fixed their B-24 in Italy.

The first problem was to get the nose jacked up. No small problem in itself. The jacking point was resting on the ground underneath the nose. We had to dig a trench under the nose to get to it. The ground was hard packed almost like cement and the only tools we had were a couple of GI trenching shovels. We all took turns and finally dug a trench to the jack-pad. The only jack we could find was a small 2-ton truck jack that could move about 6 inches. The Staff Sergeant scrounged around the landing strip and found a bunch of railroad ties and a small Japanese two-handed carpenter's saw.

We'd jack the nose up a few inches and then block it up with short pieces of railroad tie, cut by that little carpenter's saw. A slow process, but we finally got the nose up high enough to drop the gear down. Fortunately, the backside of the down-lock was still in place and undamaged. By looping cargo tie-down cables around the topside of the nose-gear strut, above its pivot, and running them back through the nose-gear access panel in the front cabin bulkhead, we could fasten them down to several D-rings on the cabin floor. With the torn-up nose gear doors removed, shredded sheet metal trimmed away and new hydraulic steering lines installed, it worked like a charm. The nose-gear wouldn't retract, but at least we could fly our bird.

After four days, we carefully taxied out and took-off for Tachikawa, the big repair depot outside of Tokyo. There I made one of my smoothest landings ever and then very cautiously let the nose wheel touch down. Darned if the whole jury rig didn't work as advertised. The engineers at Tachi took one look at our handy-work and just shook their heads. But we had saved one $550,000 C-119 for Uncle Sam.

On Thanksgiving Day I made a fast run to Korea. The weather was excellent. I was flying my own 132, the fastest bird in our squadron, and I really pushed her so we could get back to a real turkey dinner at Ashiya. We were making over 235 miles per hour, which was considerably above the normal 180 mph "corridor" cruising speed for the C-54s.

We got back in time and our turkey dinner was really something special. I counted over 32 different items on the menu. A few that I can remember were: shrimp cocktail, turkey soup, ham, roast beef, turkey, dressing, corn, peas, potatoes, head lettuce with dressing, Waldorf salad, mince pie, pumpkin pie, fruit cake, ice cream, candy and nuts. Oh yes, and a cigar. We didn't exactly suffer and were really glad we had pushed ol' 132 to make it in time.

All was not work during the Airlift. On the 29th of November I got in from flying rather early and was greeted with the news that Phil Martin and I were going on R&R (Rest & Recuperation) to the Fuji View Hotel not far to the Southwest of Tokyo. I asked when we were going, thinking they meant in a week or two. I was informed that they meant early next morning.

What a shock that was. On the airlift we normally wore our obsolete Olive-Drab uniforms (the USAF had only recently switched to Blues), but when off base we were supposed to dress up in our new uniforms. My blues on that day weren't pressed, I had only one clean blue shirt and it was still four days to payday.

A full blown party in the living room of our BOQ #47 at 2200. I don't believe Barboorosa and his "Gitfiddle" moved from the spot all day.

All through my time on the Airlift I kept my flying pay and sent home all the rest. For my family it was a system that worked pretty well, although I was never loaded with cash. However, we made it. We got up at 0230, dashed down to the 62nd Squadron Operations for our ride to Tachikawa and caught the plane just as it was starting to taxi out. We had breakfast at Tachi.

From Tachi we took a train, for about 2 1/2 hours, to the little town of Fujiyoshida near the base of Mt. Fuji. Thence, we went by bus to our hotel about five miles out of town. Our trip was through some of the most picturesque geography I have ever seen. Rugged hillsides broken up by terraced rice paddies, small villages and lots of trees. The Japanese are very efficient in the use of their very limited land, which is basically very rugged. Any small piece of level land—even 10x20 feet—would be cultivated, usually turned into a rice paddy. There are many rivers in Japan and because of the hills and mountains, the rivers are quite turbulent and pretty. They also supply an immense amount of hydroelectric power, the chief source of energy in this country.

The Fuji View is a fairly small, but very picturesque, hotel on the lower slopes of Fujiama. It has large grounds on the shore of a lake with boating, horseback riding, tennis courts and all kinds of activities. We even had movies at night.

Being in the middle of the week, as well as off-season, meant that the place was quite empty. There were seven of us from Ashiya, as well as one other officer and two Civil Service gals from Tokyo. I estimated that there were eight people operating the hotel for each guest. Needless to say the service was excellent.

The first morning, we woke up to find that it had been snowing quite hard. We ended up with about 10 inches of beautiful snow. Partly because of the weather and partly because we wanted to see more of the place, we went back to Tokyo until Friday and when we returned to the Fuji View the snow was gone and there were a few more guests. On the fifth of December we were back at Ashiya. I landed about 1030, got about one hour of sleep and was airborne for Korea by 0300.

At this point in time, the UN forces were really taking a beating. The entire energy of the C-119s was to support the Marines and Army units that were completely surrounded by several hundred thousand Chinese troops up around the Chosen Reservoir. It was very discouraging to say the least. The 314th was working full out every day, but there was no complaining. A few days earlier if we'd taxi out for takeoff, check our magnetos and found we had a 100 RPM mag drop, we wouldn't take off. With this heavy push on, if we checked the mags and the engines kept running, we'd go and no bitching either. But no complaints. Everyone was just damn glad to help those poor guys up there at the Frozen Chosen.

We were also running out of spare 110 volt inverters that powered our dual set of electric flight instruments. Normally we had a primary and stand-by inverter for the pilot's instruments and a third for the copilot's side. Being new for the AF, they were not readily available. More than once I departed Ashiya with one operational inverter and prayed that I didn't end up having to make an approach on needle, ball and airspeed. I never did, but the threat was still there.

One day at 0300 I drove off to war, but didn't quite make it. Because it was still dark when we got to our area, we landed at Hamhung, our one and only decent sized airstrip remaining in North Korea. A week before we had six. The Marines had dug out a very small dirt strip up by the Chosen Reservoir primarily to evacuate the wounded. A C-47 could squeeze in, but not a Boxcar.

Hamhung is about forty miles up the East Coast of North Korea from Wonsan. After it got light, we formed up a three-ship formation and taxied out to takeoff for our drop zone about 15 minutes away. For repeated dropping of supplies, we had long since removed and stored the rear clamshell doors and flew with the back-end of the cabin wide open. On the runway I gave it the needle for take off and, through a malfunction of our equipment, the entire load broke loose, slid out the back end of our bird and dumped 8,000 pounds of supplies right in the middle of the runway. Like I said, we didn't quite make it to the war that day.

December 6th was another day of dropping supplies to the troops surrounded up at the Chosen Reservoir. They now had all the food, gasoline and ammunition they needed. The C-47s operating out of the overgrown cow pasture up there had evacuated all the wounded and the dead. The Marines had regrouped all their forces and, on this date they started down the valley toward Hamhung about 45 miles away. Using their own artillery, plus the bombs, napalm, rockets and machine guns of hundreds of UN fighter planes they planned to literally blast their way down to the one, small, very strongly defended 20 mile diameter beachhead at Hamhung. As we know now, this maneuver was one of the classic evacuations of all time.

It was during this period that the C-119 proved its worth and also was one of the reasons why the Korean Airlift was so much bigger and a more complex operation than the earlier and much better publicized Berlin Airlift. It was the Boxcar's ability to easily airdrop at least four tons of supplies in one pass into a small area. We had 50,000 to 60,000 troops in the Reservoir area. The Airlift, thanks to complete and overwhelming air superiority, was not only able to completely resupply the Marines and other UN troops while they reorganized, but to also keep them supplied as they "advanced in a new direction" towards Hamhung. The Airlift permitted them to take all of their artillery, heavy equipment, tanks and trucks with them. Nothing of value was left behind.

Keep in mind that the Chinese had available hundreds of thousands of troops and our forces were completely surrounded. But the Chinese had no heavy weapons or airpower to hold back the Marines and their friends. At one point, as our troops advanced down that valley, the Chinese demolished a key highway bridge across a ravine. The C-119s simply airdropped by parachute a complete Treadway Bridge to the Marines who used it to span the ravine and bring out all of their heavy equipment. During those few days, all the rulebooks went out the window. For example, one C-47 out of Kimpo carried two Napalm tanks shackled under his wing. When he completed his mission he'd look up a concentration of Chinese and drop his Napalm on them. Another C-47 had dropped his supplies to an isolated unit up near the reservoir when he noticed that another unit of Marines had been chased out onto the frozen ice of a small lake with a large group of Chinese in hot pursuit. The C-47 pilot dove his plane down onto the deck and with his prop tips inches off the ice buzzed back and forth through the Chinese troops until the Marines made good their escape.

The 7th of December was kind of a novel experience for us all, after the events of the past few days. Our Squadron had only a one-plane milk run to Kimpo and back. And on the 8th we only had two aircraft committed. Combat Cargo Command, after dropping supplies like crazy to the Xth Corps, was asked to stop. They had too much and everything came to a screeching halt. The withdrawal south was getting our people into the area, once again, with good roads, ports and railroads and it just wasn't necessary to fly them in any more. On the 9th we were back to routine flying of cargo around in Korea once again and even had 0900 takeoff times.

By this time I had about 370 hours in the Charlie 119 (averaging over 110 hours per month) and felt very comfortable flying it. My total military time was getting close to 3,000 hours.

Our "routine" flying didn't last very long. On the 10th we began evacuating Kimpo as the Chinese, with their overwhelming manpower, continued to push us further south. We were pulling the fighter outfits out before the Chinese overran the place. It was heartbreaking, after almost 3 months, to see all the work being undone. The outfit we pulled out, on this day, was making its third evacuation in less than two weeks. It was the same gang I lived with after I folded up the nose-gear up at Sinanju. Two weeks before they had gotten chased out of there back to Pyongyang, then from there to Kimpo and on this day we took them back to Japan. We prayed we would not have to take them any further.

On the 13th, we started to evacuate the Hamhung Perimeter. The Marines broke through from the Chosen Reservoir, the last of them came through the night before and it was now time to close up shop up there. It was a max effort to get out as much equipment as possible. One load I had was three vehicles to go to Pusan. The last one in was the staff car of a South Korean general—it was his pride and joy. As we strapped it down in its place the trunk hung out of the back of our plane. He was in tears as we taxied out with his car hanging out the back of our C-119.

We were making as many round trips as possible, in order to get out all the supplies we could in the little time we had. All supplies and things that could not be removed were being demolished. It was not pleasant to see our side put in a position like that, but it was being accomplished in good order and as "Doug" said, "the morale of the troops was high." The previous night the demolition teams started to blow up ammunition dumps and our guys stationed there for "Comical" Cargo Command panicked, thinking the Chinese had broken through our lines. They came streaming out of their tent, half dressed and armed to the teeth with Tommy Guns and Carbines and heading for the flight line to be near the airplanes in the event a hasty exit was in order.

On one of my shuttles between Hamhumg and Pusan we were on top of an overcast, at night, on IFR down the East Coast of Korea—about 125 miles of which was enemy-held territory. As I listened on the radio I realized that the aircraft ahead of us were all stacked up over Pusan making IFR approaches and causing extensive delays. About twenty minutes out, I located a large hole in the undercast, and, even though it was night, I could easily see the surf breaking on the beach in the moonlight. I peeled off and found that there was plenty of ceiling and visibility underneath and went Visual Flight Rules the remaining way to Pusan.

All the birds ahead of us were C-54s and I was flying the lead ship of several C-119s behind me from the 61st Squadron. I promptly passed the word to my squadron mates and they all came down through that hole in the undercast and went VFR into Pusan. We landed, unloaded and were on our way back to Hamhung for another load before the guys who had been ahead of us had even started their instrument approaches. They were following their orders, but, under the circumstances, not using very good judgment.

On the 16th we completed the job of evacuating Hamhung (K-27). I was flying ol' 132 for the first time since Thanksgiving. We were one of the last dozen planes to leave. The 61st lost its first plane that night. Lt. Aldrich took off in #336 from K-27 and within a couple of minutes lost all oil from one engine. He feathered it and came back in and landed all OK. They then figured they could off-load the cargo, refill the oil tank and use that engine for about three minutes for take off. Then they planned to feather the engine again and proceed to Pohang (K-3) or Wonsan (K-9) on one engine, land and pull an engine change. However, at about that time #121 broke an elevator hinge and they decided to pull one from 336 to make 121 flyable. With only a couple of hours to go before they abandoned Hamhung, they quickly removed radio boxes and all other loose equipment possible, opened up the fuel drains and tossed in a match. It made quite a fire, fed by 1600 gallons of 145 octane gasoline. As usual 132 gave me no problems.

Having been the last one in our squadron to fly on the evacuation detail, I did no flying the next couple of days. This gave me a chance to finally get a haircut, catch up on some other details and even join in a squadron party in our living room. On the 19th I was supposed to take a routine trip to Korea, but was surprised to find, when I got to Operations, that Major McNulty had decided to take my place. I should not have been surprised. The weather was clear as a bell. I didn't see him volunteer to take anyone's place last week when the pressure was on and the weather lousy.

This guy fascinated me. A couple of days before, he called an officer's meeting. In it he gave us a long spiel about making up our minds that we would be in Japan at least for the winter and that we should settle down for a permanent stay. What amused us all was that his BOQ (one of three) was the only one that had made no effort to "move in" and fix up their quarters. He ended up by *ordering* us all to have high morale. By contrast our BOQ had built, furnished and stocked a great little bar in one corner of our living room and it was open 24 hours a day to anyone coming in off a trip. Enough about this sad excuse for an officer.

By the 20th we were practically back to stateside duty: I was the only Instrument Check Pilot without extra duties or grounded at the time, so I started giving instrument reviews and check rides. On this day I flew 2 hours and never got out of the local flying area. We also started regular ground school classes. For the first time since leaving Nashville we were just like stateside duty.

The biggest news of the day was that the 61st had a new CO. McNulty returned stateside and Colonel Diltz was his replacement. I liked Col. Diltz and presumed that there would be many changes in our squadron over the next couple of weeks. For the first time since leaving Alaska I had actually met my CO. I, along with several others in our squadron, never was introduced to McNulty.

Aerial Resupply

1951

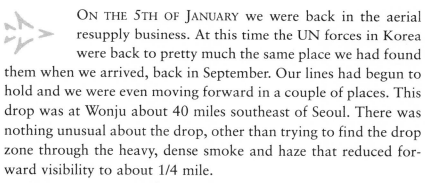ON THE 5TH OF JANUARY we were back in the aerial resupply business. At this time the UN forces in Korea were back to pretty much the same place we had found them when we arrived, back in September. Our lines had begun to hold and we were even moving forward in a couple of places. This drop was at Wonju about 40 miles southeast of Seoul. There was nothing unusual about the drop, other than trying to find the drop zone through the heavy, dense smoke and haze that reduced forward visibility to about 1/4 mile.

We got up at 0330 for the mission and got back in time for a big Review to present our 314th TC Group with its Presidential Unit Citation. It was the very first one handed out to a unit in our then new USAF. I am proud of that award and feel that we really earned it.

On the 10th of January our whole crew flew together in our own #132 for the first time in a couple of months. The weather was poor, so we flew single ships on instruments to Taegu and then dead reckoned the last 75 miles to where we thought Chung-jo was and made our letdown through the undercast. We had no navigation aids to help. When we got down to where we could see, we saw nothing but 3,500 foot hills and a few villages. In this part of Korea one hill looked like all the others. We were below the hills looking for our drop zone which was to be identified by a small white schoolhouse. After tooling around for about 30 minutes we realized we were about 25 miles behind the enemy lines.

We wheeled around and eventually found our schoolhouse. There was one small problem, however. There were no identifying signal panels on the ground. Our unit had been pushed south out of the area. We established a rectangular search pattern and eventually found a Korean soldier in the middle of a small field waving a small white flag on the end of a stick. He had the correct panels laid out on the ground and we delivered the supplies they had requested. But what a way to make a living. Everyone had a hard time on this mission. Lt Hoose, in his wanderings, finally saw a large town ahead, which turned out to be Seoul—70 miles behind the lines. We all, eventually, found our DZ and delivered our loads, but it wasn't easy. On the second day the visibility was still poor in snow showers. One of our guys (McLarnon I think) got the idea of circling the DZ with his landing lights turned on and his big Command Set keyed on to give the rest of us a radio fix to home in on. It wasn't fancy, but it worked.

For the next several days we continued our resupply drops at Chung-ju. I'll describe the 12 January trip, a typical mission. First, we had removed the big clamshell doors from the aft end of the cabin leaving the whole back-end of the cabin wide open. Then we anchored special racks of rollers to the cabin floor, so the loads on their pallets with attached parachutes could easily be pushed out the back of the plane.

In the meantime, our Airborne friends had been stacking their supplies on 4x4 foot plywood pallets. These could be ammunition, rations, gasoline or whatever else might be needed by the troops up on the line. A parachute was attached to the top of each bundle of supplies and there were usually four bundles to a pallet.

On this particular trip I will fly ol' 132 with Morton and Mathis of my regular crew. Lt. Sandidge, who I knew from Alaska, will be in the right seat. We also have an Airborne "kicker" to help with dropping the load. We are carrying 12,000 pounds of 105 mm. artillery shells. I reported to Operations one hour before takeoff to get briefed on weather, the drop zone and radio frequencies and etc. Then it is out to the airplane for pre-flight inspection, checking with Sgt. Morton about any late changes in the status of 132 and then going over radio procedures with Sgt. Mathis. Then we all go aboard and carefully check the lashing down of the load. This is now a touchy subject with me, after having dropped that load on the runway a few weeks earlier up at Hamhung.

Everything checks out OK and we climb into our Mae West life jackets and parachute harnesses and strap the airplane to our fannies. Then we fire up the engines, taxi out and take off for a routine "Corridor" flight to Taegu in Korea. Halfway across the Sea of Japan the clouds break up and it is clear and cold for the rest of the flight. At Taegu we depart from the "corridor," or regular airway, and head cross-country directly toward the Drop Zone about 75 miles away. About 15 minutes out, Sandidge passes the word to Morton and the Airborne guy to remove the tie-down cables that have held our load in place so far. For the remainder of the trip, the pallets will be held back only by the two wide web belts that go around the back end of the pallets. This web has a bomb shackle to be released when we are ready to drop the load. On the pilot's signal, the shackle was released over the DZ permitting the pallets to roll-out the back-end of the plane.

Up in the "front office" Sandy and I carefully check the snow-covered hills ahead of us against our maps to make certain that we don't miss the Drop Zone. Sure enough, dead ahead of us we see Al Ewart in #345 (the ship ahead of us) coming up out of the valley where the DZ is located.

We contact the Controller, located at the DZ right alongside a small airstrip, and get permission to enter the traffic pattern and drop our load. Our pattern is much like a normal landing pattern except we maintain 600-700 feet of altitude over the DZ. There are so many brightly colored parachutes from previous drops that there is no sweat identifying the DZ. Of course, if you look closely, to the right, you can see a couple of chutes in the middle of the Han

River, no doubt dropped by someone from the 50th Squadron. In our Squadron, we refer to them as "the 50th Communist Resupply Squadron" because they have missed the DZ so often.

Now after a couple of small heading corrections, we head directly over the DZ. As we cross the near edge of the DZ, I called the signal, Sandy hit the alarm button, Morton and the Airborne Kicker released the shackle. I applied full power, while pulling the aircraft's nose up and, in nothing flat, the 12,000 pounds of howitzer ammunition was floating down onto the DZ under their parachutes. Our mission was a success and, except for the return flight, over.

For the next couple of weeks we continue our mixed routine of cargo runs and aerial resupply drops. The cargo runs are OK, but we prefer the resupply drops. A round trip for a drop takes about one third the elapsed time of a cargo run. On one trash run (we are often referred to as Trash Carrier Command, rather than Troop Carrier Command) during this period, I was gone twenty-seven hours out of which I actually flew five.

My flight on the 27th stirred up a little excitement. I gave Lt. Childs a route check aimed at making him a First Pilot. All went well, so on the return leg to Ashiya, I took the left seat. The enroute weather was perfect and about half way home Childs asked me if I had ever had a nose wheel shimmy in a Boxcar. I said I had and described it to him. On landing at Ashiya I eased the nose wheel down and a hydraulic line blew to the nose wheel permitting a violent shimmy to occur. I slapped on the binders fast and hard (no-anti skid brakes in those days) and came to a screeching halt on the runway after blowing the four main gear tires. The shimmy was so violent that most of the avionics boxes were torn out of their shock mounts, the two pilot's instrument panels came out of their shock-mounts and were leaning back against the control columns and the big CO_2 bottle was ripped off the cockpit wall. As we came to a halt and the dust was settling down, Childs reached over, tapped me on the right shoulder and calmly said, "I didn't ask for a demonstration." If he had blown his whole check ride earlier, right then and there he'd have passed just for being so cool under pressure.

About this time we retook Suwon, about 40 miles SE of Seoul. I also read in the AF Times that I had been promoted to Captain. On the 1st of February I flew into Suwon with a few rounds of artillery shells. There were no navigation aids north of Taegu and there was a 500 foot ceiling at Suwon. We got under the overcast south of Suwon, found the railroad going to Suwon and did the first legal buzz job I'd had in a long time. The devastation on the ground was disheartening. After our retreat south through the area and then the Chinese retreat north, there was nothing of value left. And on this day, the Korean refugees, in their flowing white robes, were already starting to make their way back north walking along the railroad tracks. The refugee problem was the most pitiful thing about this whole war.

While waiting to take off at Suwon, a C-54 landed in front of us. Just as he put his nose wheel down on the runway, an ambulance drove out onto the runway directly in front of the plane. The main gear straddled the ambulance, but it collapsed the nosewheel. The vehicle was demolished—nothing higher than the top of the engine—and the C-54 was on its nose, a total loss. The aircraft crew wasn't even scratched, and even more amazing was the fact that, although unconscious, the driver wasn't really hurt either. Talk about luck!

For the next few days our life was pretty routine. Our morale was not great because we could see no end to our duty in the Far East. The C-119s had made themselves indispensable to the varied requirements of Combat Cargo Command. No replacement crews were coming in from Sewart and many of our senior staff officers seemed to go back to the States for one reason or another. Ray Hewitt and I were given the thankless job of checking out the few remaining non-first pilots in our squadron.

During this period I also got a new assignment in the squadron. There had been a couple of mix-ups in scheduling and making takeoff times, so it was decided to have a Captain/Pilot on duty at all times in Operations. I made the team, which meant 24 hours on duty in Operations and four days off. In actual practice we were only off the next day and we flew on the other days. Because the five of us made up the schedules, we pretty much had our pick of the missions. This duty also kept us off all the other extra duty rosters, so there were some advantages.

One afternoon, the fellows in our BOQ #47 decided to hold a "Martini Hour" at the bar in our living room. As things will under circumstances like this, one thing led to another and when I returned from supper the "hour" had led into the beginning of several consecutive hours and turned out to be one of those good spontaneous parties that our BOQ likes to throw. We never charged for a drink at our bar and when someone felt he had consumed a bottle's worth of liquor he simply replaced it. We knew there were a couple of deadbeats that we carried, but it wasn't worth the hassle of keeping books or losing the congenial atmosphere of our place. This was quite a contrast to the atmosphere in the Field Grade BOQ next door. One night I was invited over there to have a drink and had to pay for it. I never went back there, socially, again.

There was always a lot of rivalry between our 61st Squadron and the 50th. However, all C-119 drivers were united against the guys flying the "Gold Plate Jobs" as we called the C-54s. Lt. Childs had a couple of friends manning the local area radar station. One time when they came to visit Childs, they swore us (in our BOQ) to secrecy about a little procedure we could enjoy if we didn't spread the word around outside our little group. If the traffic was stacked up in weather at Fukuoka and Ashiya, we could contact them and they would give us radar vectors out of the "corridor" and around traffic and put us right off the end of the runway at Ashiya. This saved us all kinds of flying time and totally confused the guys, especially from the 50th, who knew they were ahead of us in the corridor and found us on the ground when they landed. When they queried us, all we ever said was that it was easy if you knew what you were doing.

The ill feeling towards the C-54s came from an incident with the C-54 outfit at Tachikawa six weeks prior to the full 314th TC Group coming to Japan. We sent four planes, one from each squadron, on ahead to get familiar with the area and operations. They were attached to the C-54 group at Tachi until the rest of us arrived. Captain Hill, from our squadron, was talking to their Operations Officer one day right after their arrival in Japan. Their Ops guy suggested that with only one crew per C-119, it might be a good idea to check out some of his C-54 pilots (they had 2 1/2 crews per plane) in our birds to take some of the load off our 8 pilots. Hill thought that was a great idea and indicated that some of our guys probably would like to check out in the C-54. The Ops guy said, "Well, we couldn't check any of you out because we have a minimum requirement of 250 hours as copilot before we let any-one ride in the left seat." Hill, quick as a flash, said, "Well, in that case, as of right now there is a minimum requirement of 250 hours as copilot for the C-119. Also, for your information, in spite of the fact we only have two engines our planes carry just as heavy a load as yours, are faster and a lot more complicated to fly." Our pilots did all the C-119 flying during that six-week period.

When we first started the air dropping of supplies, our drop zone was a huge set of frozen rice paddies about one mile wide and about three miles long. As we became more proficient, the drop zones got ever smaller. On the 14th of February they called several of us out for an emergency drop to some of our troops sur-rounded in the little town of Chipyang-ni, about 65 miles east of Seoul.

The weather was lousy at Ashiya, with 1/4 mile visibility and zero ceiling, but forecast to be OK by the time we reached the Drop Zone. We were solid instruments for about an hour and a half, then we had good weather the rest of the way. After a little looking around, we spotted our town, our friendly troops and our DZ which consisted of a small light plane strip about 100 feet wide and 1,500 feet long right, in the center of the town. Up to this point our smaller DZs had been about one mile long.

From our standpoint, the bad part of the drop, aside from the small size of the DZ, was that the Chinese infested the hills surrounding the town. If we didn't drop our load of ammunition and rations right into the DZ, they would likely fall into the hands of the Chinese, which was frowned on. We weren't too concerned about small arms fire because our fighters were working over the area and the Chinese had a lot of respect for our fighter aircraft. As we circled down over the DZ, we could see that the whole town, with the exception of one stone church, was completely burned out. We could see our troops walking around, apparently completely unconcerned about their predicament, out in the streets and gawking up at us as we circled down.

As we set up our final approach and came down to drop altitude, we had to pass close to a hill we knew was occupied by enemy troops. We thought sure we would pick up small arms fire, but nothing happened so we settled down to make a good drop right down the center of the strip. Fortunately there was almost no wind blowing, and at the signal our load went out without any trouble. As usual, I added power to assist the load going out the back of our plane. Because of the situation on the ground, we had a little extra incentive to get out of there, so I really put it into high blower. It was a good thing too, because at that point we heard the thwack of a couple of rounds of small arms fire hitting my almost new airplane.

I rolled into a steep climbing turn and really got out of there in a hurry. As we turned, I could look back and see our load settling down on either side of the strip and about 2/3 the length of the runway. A bulls-eye! When we got back home we discovered two holes in our right wing and became the first plane in our squadron to be damaged by ground fire.

On the 21st of March the 314th TC Group staged over to Taegu for our second big Airborne Troop Drop of the 187th RCT. The 1st Cavalry was moving so fast that they took the originally scheduled drop zone before we could get off the ground. So we reorganized and later went to another DZ further north.

This was a delightful mission for me. Colonel Diltz is still fairly new to the C-119 and prefered to have an instructor pilot ride with him. I flew IP for him. He was an excellent pilot and would listen to his crew if they had a suggestion to offer. I've never seen a better-led formation. He completely briefed all of our squadron pilots on exactly how he planned to lead our formation. Our times for Takeoff, Departure Point, Initial Point and over the DZ were

#132, the Queen of the Fleet at Kimpo

right on. All I had to do was observe and take some good photographs. He was a real pleasure to ride with and a total contrast to our previous CO who, while chastising us all to fly "the way he used to in the Eagle Squadron," didn't have any idea about how to lead a large formation.

Leading a large formation is an art. For example, Col. Diltz started his form-up with the leading Squadron with a nice easy 20 degree bank that never varied and we rolled out right in our proper position. McNulty never was able to judge his form-up with another squadron. He would start out with a nice bank, but would steepen it up, as he went around, to get into the correct interval. I have been on his lower wing in a 60 to 70 degree bank, almost stalled out, as he tried to adjust his position. This is not easy to do in a big transport. He never could think beyond his own aircraft. Diltz made formation flying a piece of cake.

After the drop, about half way back to Taegu, one of our C-119s from another squadron caught fire and blew up shortly after the crew bailed out. The Crew Chief of that plane was all set to jump, when he suddenly remembered that his little dog—who always flew with him—was still up in the cockpit. He ran back, got his dog, tucked him into the front of his flight jacket and made his jump OK. A real hero in our book.

The 29th of March was a sad day for the 61st Squadron. Our "Big Moose" Johnson was killed trying to crash-land his C-119 in a rice paddy on his way back from a resupply mission in Korea. At the time, we didn't know what had happened other than that the right engine simply fell off. Moose was killed when they skidded across the rice paddy and hit a stone wall on the far side. This folded the nose under the aircraft and got the pilots. The copilot was alive, but in critical condition. Sergeant Kmeic, the Crew Chief, was the one with me at K-29 when I collapsed the nose gear. He and the Radio Operator got out OK. Moose was our squadron's Chief Pilot and was the best man and officer in our squadron. I personally had a lot of respect for him and considered him my best friend during the Airlift. He originally checked me out at Sewart and was to have given me my instrument check-ride the afternoon he died. A great guy.

Later that same day, a second C-119 had its right engine fall off. Two in one day seemed a little much, so they grounded our planes. And we stayed grounded for a month before we got all our parts in from the states to modify our engine mounts by beefing them up. It turned out, later, that what we thought was the problem, really wasn't the problem at all.

A few weeks later, after we got flying again, one of our Boxcars was returning from Korea with an extra pilot dead-heading down in the cabin. Suddenly, there was a big jolt and both engines fell off and we had a big C-119 glider. This extra pilot recalled that he was certain that something went through the cabin just as this all happened. Shortly thereafter another of our pilots had a rough running engine and quickly feathered the engine. When he got it on the ground they discovered that one of the hollow steel propeller blades was almost completely severed about 18 inches in from the prop tip.

The real culprit was not the engine mounts, but prop blades. Mostly from operating out of gravel strips the face of the blade would get scored by a rock and a fatigue crack would develop and spread until the prop tip tore off and the imbalance would tear the engine off the plane. In the case of both engines coming off at the same time, combined with the third pilot's recollection, it was agreed that the right engine prop tip came off, went through the cabin and hit the prop on the left side and we had an instant glider. After that, prop blades were an important part of our preflight inspections.

During that down month we did all kinds of things to keep ourselves busy, such as special ground school classes. I started a class in photography and, during this period, General MacArthur got recalled. The 61st easily walked off with top inspection honors for the group and Colonel Henderson gave our squadron a three-day pass for all kinds of squadron activities and recreation. We had fishing trips, bus trips to Fukuoka and Kokura, a beer bust and picnic on the beach. Naturally Colonel Diltz was delighted.

On the 19th of April the 61st got the first aircraft back in the air in almost exactly four weeks. I was at the controls because I was overdue for an instrument check. It was good to get back in the air again, but I was sure rusty. I gave Hill a lousy ride during the first half of my ride, but during the last half I got back into the swing of it and I got a passing grade.

On the 26th of April I flew my first trip to Korea since our planes became grounded. Chris and I flew a load of ammunition up to Kimpo, outside of Seoul. What a mess Kimpo was. Only the one short runway was usable. The main runway had 167 craters in it. Almost all of the buildings had simply disappeared. In front of the big white administration building there was one new addition—the burned-out hulk of a Russian built T-34 tank. It apparently had been caught there when we retook Kimpo. I didn't know it when I was there, but the Chinese were only 10 miles north of the field, once again, and shortly after our departure they evacuated Kimpo for the third time.

A burned out Russian-made T-34 tank in front of the administration building at Kimpo 26 April 1951.

On the 30th of April I had one of my most amazing trips to Korea. Paul Hendrix and I had a 0110 takeoff for Kimpo. We had a maximum effort of airlifting artillery ammunition into Kimpo. Because of the takeoff time, combined with the fact that Paul and I had only had about two or three hours of sleep the night before, we had a large steak at the club. We also borrowed a two-gallon thermos and had it filled with coffee. With these important things accomplished we made our weary way out to the flight line a little before midnight. The weather was excellent and quite in contrast to the rain of the previous few days.

The Chinese were still in their big offensive mode and had pushed down along the east side of the Han River, with the intent of retaking Kimpo. Our forces were using artillery and naval gunfire to keep them from crossing the Han River. Our job was to help keep the artillery supplied with ammunition.

With full stomachs, a full load of ammo and a full jug of coffee, we took off and had a very pleasant trip to Kimpo. Because of fairly strong headwinds we landed at 0330. As we approached Kimpo the sights were almost unbelievable. About 100 miles out from Kimpo we could begin to see the flashes from the artillery fire. At that point it looked a lot like summertime heat lightning. As we got closer, we could see on the ground the lights of long truck convoys heading north and, occasionally, a train rumbling along the railroads that our troops had blown up and rebuilt so many times. Incidentally, a train was almost never seen in North Korea, because of our air interdiction program.

As we got up near Kimpo, the flash of the artillery fire and the orange bursting of their shells was one of the most awesome sights I have ever seen. To make the whole thing even more weird, the whole area was illuminated by star shells, big million candlepower flares dropped from aircraft on parachutes, as well as from huge concealed searchlights on the ground. It was truly the devil's playground.

When we finally got on the ground, after making a close pattern to keep away from the Han River, the booming and whomphing of the artillery was almost continuous. The Chinese mortars were probing to within about a mile or so of Kimpo. From our plane you could see the tracers from our automatic weapons going into their positions. Huge flares continually kept the battlefield illuminated and outlined the mountains surrounding the area and kept everything bathed in a weird flickering light. Most of the planes unloaded in about twenty minutes to a half hour. Through some mix-up a couple of us, including my plane, were there for over an hour and a half. By the time we took off it was beginning to get daylight so we kind of took a tour down the Han—at a respectful altitude and distance, of course. We could see all along the north and east side of the river where our artillery had torn up the ground. We also saw fires where little villages were burning and then smaller fires around which, no doubt, were huddled small groups of Chinese soldiers trying to keep warm in the cold Korean weather. It really was an experience that I was never to forget.

We all kept flying regularly for the next few days. On the first of May, I made another early morning takeoff for a trash run to Kimpo and back. In contrast to my previous run up there, there was no discernible activity around Seoul that we could detect. It was almost too quiet to be true.

On the second we flew a five-ship formation up the east coast for a supply drop. Major Gilmore led the first flight and I led the second flight. The air was a smooth as glass and there was not a cloud in the sky.

On the fourth, we flew a group night formation flight that turned out to be a real rat race. Gilmore led our squadron, I led the second flight and Buckley the third. Shortly after getting airborne GCA (Ground Controlled Approach) asked us for a practice run for a formation on GCA. That did it! Gilmore forgot to tell us which channel to switch our radios to. At one point GCA told us to put our landing gear down and apparently I was the only one to hear it. My two wing men almost ran past me when my gear came down and Buckley had to turn his flight off to keep from over riding us. After landing we had to abort our #132 because we had blown a large hole in our right hand exhaust manifold. Buckley told us later that he flew formation for 20 minutes with the town of Osaka before he realized it wasn't the rest of the formation. He realized his mistake and looked for the rest of the formation. He spotted them off to one side and below and led his formation down to join up again. These lights turned out to be six fishing boats on the Sea of Japan.

On the 11th we made a most interesting drop, and it turned out to be my last one on the airlift. It was on the very peak of a rugged 5,000-foot mountain on the eastside of Korea. If it hadn't been for a "Mosquito Controller" in his T-6 we never would have found our DZ. The whole eastcoast of Korea is made up of rugged hills and they all look alike. The UN guys were pushing the Chinese North and couldn't get their supplies quickly enough over this essentially trackless terrain. So Combat Cargo flew them in.

This ability of the UN forces to resupply by air, and at will, was the prime factor that permitted us to turn the tide against

China's unlimited man power. Their lines were extended, we dominated the air and their supplies had to be delivered on the backs of their troops. Their trucks were continuously being destroyed and their trains couldn't move. It was interesting to learn, years later, that it was actually less expensive for us to deliver supplies by air than it was to truck them up from the south. Aerial resupply also made logistical planning a lot simpler. In an emergency, we could have supplies on the ground where they were needed within four hours of our getting the call. Even to the troops on the front line.

This drop on the top of the 5,000-foot mountain, was one of those emergency drops. We dropped, flying south to north, right onto the peak of the mountain and it was the smallest DZ, for me, to date. The instant we dropped our load we wracked into a steep climbing left turn, because the Chinese were on the next mountain. One advantage to a quick climbing turn is that we could look back and see our load coming down right on target. It was a fruitful and most satisfying mission.

And so it went for the next couple of weeks. We were flying most every day. At one point our squadron had enough planes in operation to supply one half of our group's airlift ability. On the 6th of June I had a one-week R&R back up to the Fuji View Hotel. When I returned to Ashiya I found we were still flying more than enough to keep us busy. Each plane was making at least one, and often two, trips each day. I went back to being Duty Officer at Operations every fifth day.

Our first crew to rotate back to the States left while I was on R&R and I was to go on the second crew one month later. There was an unwritten policy in our group, that anyone scheduled home was taken off of the flying schedule one week prior to his rotation. Not me, however, because I flew right up through my last day at Ashiya. Years later, I was told that it was my punishment for being a nonconformist in the Squadron. Another meaning to the phrase "small world."

On the first of July I went to Tokyo for processing back to the US. Courtesy of Pan Am I arrived at Travis AFB on the third and

I got home to Nashville on the fourth of July. It had been a long 60 days TDY

California, Here We Come

1951 TO 1953

SHORTLY AFTER RETURNING TO SEWART AFB I had the opportunity to go to the University of California—Berkeley to be an Air Force ROTC instructor. It was our first choice in location and a delightful assignment, especially after the pressure of the Airlift operations. I didn't realize it at the time, but the pressure of flying the Airlift had, for me, taken all the fun out of flying. Although I continued to fly, it was never the same again.

So Martha and I packed the two girls and our belongings into our Ford and headed for California. It was quite a trip. About Tucumcari, NM we discovered that Chris (our older daughter) had Chicken Pox, so we didn't dare stop any place over night for fear of being quarantined. Other than that and the fact that they closed Route 40, because of snow, just a few cars behind us as we went through Flagstaff, AZ, the trip was relatively uneventful.

Shortly after we reached California, we purchased our first house. It was a white stucco, California Ranch style, three-bedroom, tract home in Danville, CA. Danville is a delightful small town out in the valley about 15 miles east of Berkley in the midst of the walnut orchards. The climate was delightful and we enjoyed our stay there. Our house was located right at the foot of Mt. Diablo. You could walk out our back door and there was nothing between our house and the top of Mt. Diablo.

About the time our furniture arrived I was sent to the Instructors Course at the Command and Staff School at Maxwell AFB in Alabama. It was a very good course. While at the school, it was interesting to see how my Instructor Pilot keeps interweaving the threads of our lives. One of our guest speakers turned out to be Commander Costello, my Navy mentor from Adak, Alaska. We had a great visit and he informed me that the Navy had bought our plan for them taking over Davis AFB on Adak. This was great news for me, because I had never heard how our project up there had turned out. It was nice to learn that we had done a good job.

My assignment at Berkeley was to teach Political Geography to Freshmen. I really enjoyed this course, even though there were many times that I was only one chapter ahead of the students. I'm sure that I got more out of the course than they did. Our Detachment Commander was Col. George Steele. He was a great guy and I really enjoyed serving under him. His was a very smooth running detachment.

One morning I went downstairs from my office to my first class of the day. As I approached my classroom I noticed that Col. Steele and a civilian were standing outside the door to my class. When I walked up the Colonel introduced me to Dr. So-and-so. I acknowledged the introduction and the Col. asked me if the name was familiar. I said that it was, but couldn't place it. He said that the doctor had written the chapter in our textbook on Korea. "Isn't your class today on Korea?" The Col. went on to say that the Doctor would like to sit in on my class for a few minutes and would I mind?

I liked to have died and quickly went on to explain to him that my class today was not about his chapter in the book, but was a color slide presentation on the Korean Airlift and how America's Powerhood Factor of Technology coped with China's Powerhood Factor of Unlimited Manpower. The doctor said that that would be fine, because he could only stay about 10 minutes. We went in and he took a seat in the back of the class. To my surprise, he stayed for the whole period. He came up afterward and chatted with me and told me how much he enjoyed my presentation. He also told me that it was his first opportunity to see anything about Korea since before WW II.

While at Cal I car-pooled with Sam Lyons. We did so the whole time I was there. I would pick up Sam at his house in Lafayette, drive over the foothills and down past the Claremont Hotel and across to the campus in Berkeley. In the afternoon, after classes, Sam and I would often play handball, clean up, stop at the Claremont Hotel for a drink and then head out east into the valley and home. It was tough duty, but someone had to do it.

Being in Berkley we flew out of Hamilton AFB for our flying time. As usual I was an Instructor Pilot and Instrument Check Pilot for our detachment. Most of our flying consisted of flying regular C-47 cargo runs to Oklahoma City or an occasional "Navigational Proficiency Flight" to Las Vegas for a weekend. We had those weekend trips to Las Vegas down to a science for minimum expenses. I remember one "expensive" weekend that cost me $14 total. The biggest single item was the taxi fare from Nellis AFB into town. We knew where all the free meals were to be had and, in those days, a big casino show had a "minimum" charge of one dollar. I would order a Tom Collins and nurse it through the entire show.

Being an instructor could sometimes be an adventure. On one trip to Oklahoma City with a stop at Tucson, AZ. Col. Steele flew the first leg From Hamilton AFB to Tucson. Capt. George Barnes was in the copilots seat and I rode in the radio operators seat about ten feet behind the pilot's seat logging Instructor Pilot time. Nothing unusual was going on, so I fell asleep. The next thing I knew the Crew Chief was shaking my shoulder and waking me from a sound sleep. He told me that Col. Steele wanted to see me. Keep in mind that the Col. was only a couple of years from retirement and not the greatest pilot. Rubbing the sleep from my eyes, I went forward to see what the Col. wanted.

He wanted me to take over and do the landing, which was fine by me. I buckled myself into the pilot's seat and started to look around and see what was going on. Imagine my surprise when I found we were already all the way down on the downwind leg of the traffic pattern and ready to turn on the crosswind leg of the pattern for landing. I made the turn OK, and then discovered why the Col. wanted me to make the landing. We had a very strong crosswind on the runway and the C-47 doesn't really take kindly to strong crosswind landings. The good Col. had given me about one minute to wake up from a sound sleep and execute a difficult landing. Bless his soul. I made the landing OK, but what a way to wake up from a sound sleep.

In the summer of 1953 we held the Air Force ROTC Summer Camp at Hamilton AFB across the Bay from Berkeley. This was a very pleasant assignment and turned out to be my swan song in the Air Force. Three things stand out in my memory of that summer. First, we arranged for all of the ROTC cadets to get an orientation ride in one of the then new T-33 jet trainers. This was a real treat for the cadets, but left us Tactical Officers very jealous because we had not been included. When I pointed this out to the Base Commander, he promptly made arrangements for us to get rides in a jet also. This was my first taste of a jet aircraft and I promptly fell in love with this new technology.

The second thing that summer was that I got my first exposure to Bob Hoover, North American Aviation's famous Engineering Test Pilot. The Air Force pilots flying F-86D's out of Hamilton were complaining that the 6,000 foot runway at Hamilton was really too short for the then new F-86D All-Weather fighter. It was becoming a morale problem. The Base people talked to North American—the plane's manufacturer—and they sent Bob up to Hamilton to show the Air Force pilots a thing or two about their F-86s. The Summer Camp group was also invited down to the field to watch the show.

Bob walked out to the Flight Line and, at random, picked out an 86D from Hamilton and took it out to fly. This was obviously not a special factory demonstrator. Bob taxied out and went down the taxiway in front of us to our right. The taxiway joined the runway about 1,000 feet short of the end of the runway. Bob did his run-up checks on the end of the taxiway and then turned right to go to the end of the runway in order to take advantage of its full length. He turned into the wind, set his brakes, ran up full power and executed a maximum performance takeoff. He was airborne before he reached the taxiway, had traffic pattern altitude by the time he reached the end of the runway, went around and did a short field landing and turned off when he reached the original taxiway. All told he had used 1,000 feet of the 6,000 foot runway. There was no more complaining about Hamilton's runways being too short for the 86D.

The third thing I particularly recall about that ROTC encampment was the entertainment program we had for the final night. We had one cadet with good connections in the entertainment world in San Francisco. He persuaded us to let him make the arrangements for our entertainment that night. We told him to have at it. He showed up with two of what he felt were up and coming entertainers that were unknown to most people at that time. One was from The Purple Onion and the other was from The Hungry Eye. One of them was a young man named Harry Bellefonte. And what a show he did put on and is still one of my favorite entertainers. It was a great way to end my career in the Air Force.

In November of that year I was caught in one of Secretary of Defense Johnson's big RIFs (Reduction in Force) and I suddenly found myself unemployed. I scrambled around looking for a job and was hired as a car salesman for a Chevrolet dealer in Concord, CA. I wasn't there very long and I'm probably the only Chevrolet salesman that ever drove a Ford.

Aero Commander

1953 TO 1957

WHILE STARTING TO SELL Chevrolets I sent resumes to Aero Commander, Beech and Cessna, all of whom were just starting to produce light twin business aircraft. I was surprised to get favorable responses from all three manufacturers. I selected Aero Commander. They were young, aggressive and I thought (still do) they had the best of the original light twins. Rufe Amis (who ran a big heavy construction company) and his brothers in Oklahoma City and George Pew (Sun Oil Company family) put up the money. Ted Smith and his friends from Douglas Aircraft were the engineering and production talent behind the project. Carl Wooton, who built the Beechcraft distributor organization, headed up marketing. They were a very potent team.

Col. Steele was good enough to write letters of recommendation for me. Some months later I was shown one by Lee Renshaw, the Program Manager for the Cessna 310. The one part that I recall with amusement stated, "Capt. Conklin has spent two years selling the idea to college freshmen of making a career in the U.S. Air Force. If anyone can successfully do that, he can sell anything."

Gene Hudman and I were the first two factory sales representatives hired by Aero Commander. I covered the eleven western states and Gene covered the remaining eastern states. I found out later that I was the first applicant that Aero had talked to that had ever sold an airplane before. But what an exciting time it was for us all. Aero was small and had a hands-on management unlike Cessna and Beech the other two, long-established, competitors. We could quickly make things happen. We were the first with three bladed props, first with supercharged engines and first with a pressurized cabin, to mention a few of the items we pioneered.

Ted Smith was one of the geniuses of our business. Before leaving Douglas to help start Aero Commander, he was the project engineer on the Air Force's fabulous B-26 light bomber. Incidentally, we always referred to the B-26 as the Commander prototype because of their similar appearance. His last assignment at Douglas was to pressurize the B-26. So when he and his colleagues at Douglas were laying out the Commander, Ted was thinking pressurization and built-in all the basic structural strength needed for pressurizing the Commander. Later on, when we decided to build the Alticruiser (pressurized Commander) all the basic structure was already there. All we needed to do was add heavier gauge metal to the convex dome over the cockpit, extra structural straps between the windows, sturdier windows and adding pressure bulkheads at the front and rear of the cabin. The rest of the structure for pressurization was already in place. Ted's ability to look ahead into the future was uncanny and made him the brilliant designer he was.

Carl Wooten was a superb marketing man. He had a flair for letting the competition spend big money on some advertising campaign, stir up a lot of excitement and then with a couple of well timed ads on our part, ride in on the coat tails of all the excitement they had stirred up. This kept our advertising budget low by comparison. Carl also had a flair for getting free publicity. His best-known publicity stunt was to remove the left propeller on the original Commander prototype and have Bert Bantle and Emmet Morris fly it from Oklahoma City to Washington, DC on one engine, with appropriate photo coverage. "What's the good of having two engines if it won't fly completely on one?" Years later he told me that the old Twin Beech could have done this also, but he never could persuade anyone at Beech to try it. That one story did more to sell Commanders than any other single effort. And it didn't cost a dime in advertising money.

Carl taught me all the basics of being a professional airplane salesman. For example, always park your demonstrator where people can easily see it—like under a floodlight if parked overnight. I remember flying into a small field on the south side of Bakersfield, CA on a business call. The office I was going to was on the east end of a long row of T hangars. However, the west end was right alongside of Route 99, the main highway through the San Joaquin Valley. I parked down near the highway, so my demonstrator could be seen, and walked back to where I was going to make my call. When I returned there was a big Cadillac convertible parked next to my bird and three men in loud sport shirts and chino pants were peering into the windows of my demonstrator. They were Clyde Hall and two of his supervisors from Clyde Hall Drilling Company in Bakersfield. They were driving by and saw my plane. They had heard about the Commander, but had never seen one up close before. They had been operating a single-engine Bonanza.

Over the next few days I flew a number of typical trips for Clyde Hall. It was their habit to bulldoze a landing strip alongside any new oil well rig they were working. Then they could fly in payrolls, a supervisor, parts or whatever was needed rather than make long drives from Bakersfield. One afternoon, as we were getting ready to leave one of his wells a little west of Bakersfield, I asked Clyde if he had ever seen a short field takeoff in a Commander, which is rather spectacular—just like Bob Hoover. He said no, but would like to see one. We got in and I got into the pilot's seat, carefully telling Clyde that this was not a stunt and that we would always have single engine control speed should we ever lose an engine. I gave him a good briefing on what I was planning to do and what it would be like.

I lined up on the dirt strip, held the brakes and ran up full power. I released the brakes and as soon as we had flying speed, rotated off the strip and started to climb out with about a forty-five degree deck angle. It was quite spectacular. Clyde was impressed. However, shortly after we started to climb out I lost the right engine. I quickly cleaned up the aircraft, feathered the dead engine and headed back to Bakersfield. I was most embarrassed and apologized profusely to Clyde. He said "Don't apologize. See that little ravine down there? That's where we landed our Bonanza two weeks ago when its engine quit. Your demonstration just sold you a Commander."

Carl also insisted that Gene Hudman and I be checked out in the Commander by Emmett Morris, our chief test pilot. As a Senior Pilot and Instructor Pilot in the Air Force I thought I knew a thing or two about how to fly, but Emmitt soon showed us otherwise and how to become a smooth, precision pilot. He asked me, early in our first ride, to do a stall out of a climbing turn, which I did. "No! No! Conklin. I want that stall to come at precisely 90 degrees into the turn." Emmitt also taught us about maximum performance. At one point we were flying out of a small grass field west of Oklahoma City. Using maximum performance, he showed us a complete 800 foot traffic pattern all within the confines of that little field.

Carl also insisted that, with a customer in the airplane, we demonstrate from the right seat and let the customer fly from the left seat. Up to that time all aircraft salesmen demonstrated from the left seat, which made the aircraft look good. Carl's radical idea was to show how easy our airplane was to fly and make the customer look good. Excellent psychology. Now, everybody does it, but Carl invented the idea. I remember giving a demo ride to Jimmy Stewart the movie actor. He was a well-qualified pilot and I was glad to have him fly in the left seat. Several weeks later he was offered a demo ride in a Cessna 310 and the factory demo pilot jumped into the left seat. Jimmy looked at the demo pilot and said, "Your airplane must be too difficult for me to fly." He turned around and walked off.

Carl also invented the idea of a factory ground school and pilot check out for our aircraft. Now, of course, everyone does it, but we started the idea and the result was that our owners generally got better insurance rates. A year or so before I retired from Falcon Jet, Carl visited me at Teterboro. I took him through our classrooms with their systems mockups and our flight simulators and all and Carl couldn't believe what we all are doing today with his basic idea. It sure was a long way from the slides we projected— one on one—on Jim Watson's office wall.

Carl also remembered old friends. He, of course, knew Sid "Smiling Jack" Nesbit from his days of selling Beech aircraft at Atlantic Aviation right after World War II. In 1946 Sid, along with Bud Lathrop of Bristol-Myers and a handful of others, met at the Wings Club in New York City and formed the nucleus of what became the National Business Aviation Association. In 1952 Sid left Atlantic and disappeared from the aviation scene. About 1955 Carl found Sid as a Night Clerk in a small hotel in Toronto. Carl brought Sid back as a Regional Sales Manager where he did a bang up job for us.

It should be kept in mind that in the early 1950s the concept of a light twin business aircraft was a very revolutionary idea. We had one very experienced distributor in Texas who made a comment that, unfortunately for him, got back to us at the factory. He said that when we produced 80 aircraft he was going to drop the franchise because that was all the potential market there was for light twin aircraft. We quickly dropped him as a distributor, because we didn't need anyone with that negative an attitude. As best I can determine, Commander delivered well over 4,600 of just the short fuselage 520, 560, 500 and 680 models of the Commander. And, of course, there were all the Cessna 310s and Beechcraft Twin Bonanzas. It was a most exciting and fun time to be in our business.

When Ted Smith outlined the performance projections for the new supercharged model 680 (two 340 HP supercharged engines = 680). I was most surprised by its much better than advertised single engine performance. We knew that Ted was good, but hadn't realized he was that good. In those days the single hydraulic pump, used for the operation of the flaps and landing gear, was on the left engine. So, in demonstrating, we normally shut down the right engine so that we would have our hydraulic pump running. We actually flew that aircraft for 72 hours before we blew that left engine. You can visualize the red faces at Lycoming Engines when they tore that engine down and discovered high compression pistons had been mistakenly installed in that supercharged engine rather than the normal pistons. Lycoming engineers calculated that that one engine—for 72 hours—was producing 450 horsepower and gave us that great single engine performance. Being the first with everything was exciting, but so was the learning curve.

From 1953 to 1957 I was the Western Sales Representative for Aero Commander. I had the fun of touring the eleven western states in a nice new Commander demonstrator. I helped set up as distributors Western Commander in Southern California, Vest Aircraft (Don Vest was the original wholesaler of used aircraft) in the Colorado and Northern California areas and young Bill Boeing and his partner Jack Murdock in the Washington/Oregon area. I demonstrated our aircraft to the likes of test Pilots Tony Levere and Fish Salmon at Lockheed Aircraft, Jimmy Stewart, Bob Cummings and John Wayne.

It was while working with Bill Boeing in Seattle that I met the most charismatic person that I have known in this business. His name was Miro Slovak and he was Bill Boeing's pilot. When I first met him, his primary job was to drive Bill Boeing's racing hydroplane. He was a big hero to the kids on the street in Seattle, because of his hydroplane racing feats.

Miro was the Czechoslovakian airline pilot who, with his copilot, was the first to defect over the Iron Curtain to the West. Mrs. Boeing was from Czechoslovakia and they sponsored Miro to the United States. He was a good-looking young man and everyone liked him, especially the young ladies. He was also a great sportsman. Martha and I were watching him on TV, one time, racing Bill's hydroplane in Miami. It was a tight race with Miro fighting to maintain his slight lead. Suddenly the number two boat flipped over and with no hesitation Miro chopped off his power and circled back to pull his competitor out of the water. A real sportsman.

Over the next few years I kept loosely in touch with Miro. He left Bill and became a Captain on Continental Airlines. He also flew in the Reno Air Races and was the US distributor for the Fournier powered sailplane. The power-plant was a modified Volkswagon engine of forty horsepower that gave it a cruise speed of about 100 mph. About ten years after I knew Miro in Seattle, I was with Atlantic Aviation at Teterboro Airport in New Jersey. I looked up at our traffic pattern one day and was surprised to see one of the rare Fourniers coming in to land. I went over to check, when it parked on our ramp, and, sure enough, it was being flown by Miro. We had a good reunion and I approved a personal check for him to purchase a new artificial horizon for his bird. He was planning to fly it to London in a big handicap race from the top of the Empire State building to the top of the Tower of London.

Volkswagon of America kept their plane in our hangar. I introduced Miro to them and the upshot was that Volkswagon arranged for him to be picked up, in a Volkswagon, as he came out of the Empire State Building and delivered him to his Volkswagon Powered Fournier at Teterboro. When he finally landed at London another Volkswagon delivered him to the Tower of London. This was great publicity for both Miro and Volkswagon.

I clearly remember my ride with Tony Levere and Fish Salmon in my Commander demonstrator. Their assignment was to evaluate the Commander for Lockheed to use as an inter-plant shuttle in Southern California. They were my first exposure to really big time, famous test pilots. Beforehand, I had visions of Clark Gable in leather jacket, flowing silk scarf, terminal velocity dives and 9G pullouts in their evaluation. Tony flew in the left seat and Fish rode behind us in the cabin and hard-timed Tony all the way. Tony took off from Burbank's Lockheed Air Terminal, turned west over the San Fernando valley and checked some simple stability tests, flew it briefly on single engine. He then made a 180 degree turn and was obviously heading back to Burbank. Thinking of Clark Gable, I said, "Gee, Tony, isn't there anything else you'd like to try? Stalls? Anything?" And here he taught me something about really great pilots. His response was, "It's approved by the FAA (Federal Aviation Administration) isn't it?" When I said that it was, he responded, "Well, if it's good enough for them, it's good enough for me." He had seen what he wanted and didn't need to prove to me what a great pilot he was. It was not a wasted lesson to me.

I also had the fun of giving Bob Hoover his first ride in a Commander. I, of course, knew of Bob having seen him demonstrate the F-86D to the Air Force pilots at Hamilton AFB a couple of years previously. He and Col. Debolt (in charge of North American Aviation's international military sales) had been given the task of evaluating the Commander for NAA as an inter-plant shuttle in Southern California.

Later, after North American bought Aero Commander, Bob made the aircraft famous at air shows all around the country with his acrobatic routine in it. The company later made a promotional film of Bob's routine in the Commander. One part, that I will always remember, was photographed from the back of the cabin looking forward so that you could see the horizon go around, through the windshield, while Bob executed an aileron roll. In itself this was not too spectacular, but with Bob's flare for theatrics, he balanced an empty glass on the instrument panel glare shield, took a pitcher full of water in his right hand and poured the water into the glass while executing the roll with his left hand. He didn't spill a drop.

During this time I was asked to represent our company at a meeting in Wichita of the Flight Safety Foundation. At the end of the meeting, Beech was kind enough to fly several FAA people and myself to Tulsa to catch the airlines. Along with three FAA fellows I was assigned to ride with Marvin Small in his nice new Twin Bonanza demonstrator. On his way to Tulsa Marvin gave us his whole spiel on the Twinbo. I was the last one off the plane and, as

I shook Marvin's hand, I said to him, "I don't think you know who I'm with. I'm not FAA, I'm with Aero Commander." His reaction was, "Oh no! I gave you my whole spiel!" From then on we became good friendly competitors and our paths have crossed many times over the years since.

Minnesota

1957 TO 1962

IN THE SPRING OF 1957 Carl Wooten moved on to Trecker Aircraft in Milwaukee. The Trecker Gull was a twin engine amphibian manufactured in Italy by Piaggio and brought to this country by Fran Trecker, Chairman of Trecker Machine Tool Company. Because of its versatility of being able to fly from both land and water, Fran thought the Gull would make a good corporate aircraft. Carl and I saw the P-166 which used the Gull's wing, tail and landing gear, but had a roomy (6 ft. stand-up cabin for four passengers and an aft lavatory) land fuselage. It was flying two years before Beech's Queen Air. A year later Fran got out of the airplane business and only a handful of P-166s got delivered in thus country—mostly to Northrop Aircraft for inter-plant shuttles in the Los Angeles area.

It is a shame that this project was allowed to die, because it would have been two years ahead of Beech with a modern, medium twin-engine aircraft with a very roomy cabin. However, over the years I have observed Piaggio repeatedly and consistently bungle the marketing of a new product in this country. It is too bad because they have produced some good aircraft. As of the writing of this book, they are, for the third time, trying to reintroduce their twin-engine turboprop—the Avanti. When introduced ten years ago, the Avanti was a much better aircraft than Beech's

Starship of similar design. Because of the rapid advancements in straight jet aircraft technology, the turboprop is a dying breed of corporate aircraft. I don't think that this is an opportune time to try to bring to market a turboprop business aircraft.

In April of 1958 we closed Trecker Aircraft. In May, with an assist from Aero Commander, I was hired by the Peavey Company (then the number three grain company in Minneapolis—25,000 employees and operations extending from Canada to Kansas and from Seattle to Buffalo) to be their salesman, and later Sales Manager, for Commander in the North Central Region. Peavey also owned the Cessna Distributorship for Minnesota and Iowa. They were a very airplane oriented company, but had had serious management problems in their aviation divisions. Using Ken Osterberg, a well-known aviation consultant, they brought in John Stuber—also from California—and myself to try to straighten things out. Minnesota Airmotive was a first class fixed base operation and Minneapolis was a delightful town to live in.

After I had been with Minnesota Airmotive about a week, and had a chance to get a little acquainted, John Stuber called me into his office and asked, "How many aircraft do you think you can sell this next year?" Obviously I had been thinking about this and, as a former factory representative, was a little acquainted with the previous management's performance. I told John that I thought it would be reasonable to expect seven sales during the next twelve months. This was up somewhat from the average performance of the former group. He smiled and informed me that the previous group had left us with a backlog of 20 regular Commanders, plus three pressurized Alticruisers and we had no orders in hand. He also advised me that he didn't intend to cancel any of those factory orders. I almost died, but we went to work.

Having previously been in the aviation business in the Twin Cities John knew the companies and the people. I knew the product. We made a good team and enjoyed working together. We sold all 23 of those Commanders and actually ordered a couple more before that year was up. We even tied Western

Commander in Santa Monica, CA for first place in sales—historically they were always the top Commander distributor. We also pioneered the installation of weather radar in a number of these aircraft.

One of my all-time favorite customers is John Bean, then Vice President—International Operations for International Multifoods Corporation in Minneapolis. John owned a Cessna 310 that he based with us at Airmotive and I wanted to sell him a Commander. John was always a stickler for details and really put me through the hoops comparing my Commander with his Cessna 310. In the process I learned the basics of how to really compare aircraft. It became the basis for the kind of aircraft comparisons that are so much a part of our business today. Later, John became the first National Business Aviation Association (NBAA) Board member picked from the executive side of the membership rather than from the company pilot side of the organization. John, his wife Ruth, Martha and I have been good friends ever since.

Shortly after that year was over, I had a rather insistent phone invitation for Martha and I to have dinner with Ken Osterberg and his wife. The manner of his invitation was not to be taken lightly. When we got there we found John and Gale Stuber were there also and knew that something was up. After the dinner was over, Ken got right to the point. In essence he said, "They had a proposition for me. I didn't have to accept, but if I didn't I'd never go any further within the Peavey Company. Would I take over and run the Cessna distributorship at Fleming Field in South St. Paul?" I allowed that, under the circumstances, I would be delighted to take the job. In reality I thought it was the chance of a lifetime for an airplane salesman.

Taking over Lysdale Aviation became a very challenging job for me. Bob Lysdale had originally owned the Cessna Distributorship at Fleming Field in South St. Paul, MN. A couple of years earlier he had sold it to the Peavey Company and stayed on as their Manager. It was a combination that didn't work. Lysdale was a loner and never fit into the Peavey management scheme of things found in any large corporation. He was asked to leave and that is where I came into the picture.

One of the first things I did was to suggest a change in the company name to try to shake the Lysdale image. I was ex-Air Force and the AF mascot is the Falcon. I had also just taken delivery of one of the first 12 Ford Falcons delivered in the Twin Cities. So I dreamed up the name Falconaire Aviation. I thought the (e) on the end gave it some class. The Peavey Company liked the name also. The next thing I worked on was to build a reasonable profit into our retail aircraft sales. Lysdale had been almost giving them away. We already had an excellent engine overhaul shop and were well known for our repair of Edo floats—water operations were a big part of our retail business.

Early on at Falconaire Gordy Campbell, one of our owners, decided to acquire a set of Edo amphibious floats for his Cessna 180. Howard Humphrey, my Sales Manager, Gordy and I stood in front of our hangar door and negotiated our deal. I finally made my final offer and stood pat. Gordy said nothing for several minutes and stood tracing patterns with the toe of his shoe in the crushed bluestone on our ramp. Howard, bless his soul, also said nothing and there was total silence for several minutes. Finally Gordy said, "I'll take them." And we sent him on his way. As he drove away, Howard grabbed my arm and said, "Do you know what you just did?" I said, "No." Howard said, "You just made more gross profit on those floats than Lysdale made selling Gordy his Cessna 180." A new era had arrived at Minnesota's Cessna distributorship!

Another change that I made was to equip our twin-engine Cessna 310 demonstrator with good Collins avionics instead of the least expensive, Mickey Mouse avionics favored by my predecessor. In my years selling Aero Commanders I had learned that if a buyer of that kind of aircraft was exposed to good avionics he will want them in his own aircraft. It had the added bonus of increasing our gross sales about 15% without selling more units.

Bob Pond, another of our owners, brought his Cessna 310 to us to have a, then brand new, Distance Measuring Equipment

(DME) receiver installed in his plane. Today, Bob is well known for his antique airplane museum in California and building special racing planes for the Reno Air Races. Back then he was the VP Marketing for his father's Advance Machine Company. A DME told you, accurately, how far away you were from a radio navigation station. Bob was getting ready for an extended business trip through the eastern half of the US and wanted one of these new-fangled DMEs for his trip. We got it installed OK and sent him on his way. When he came back I asked him how he liked it. He said it was OK, but not as accurate as he had expected. I asked him to explain and he told me that he would be flying along, visually, and could see straight down as he passed over the range station. The DME would still be reading maybe one mile. When I asked him how high he was flying he said 5,000 to 6,000 feet—and suddenly the light went on. He was one mile above the station. Bob had no more complaints about the accuracy of his DME.

My immediate boss at the Peavey Company was G. A. D. (Gerry) Smith. He was the company's Chief Financial Officer. Gerry was a tough—but fair—taskmaster. His initials, incidentally, often got misspelled. However, Gerry took kindly to this young airplane salesman and taught him the ways of big corporation financial thinking. Gerry had started with Peavey as an office boy and worked his way up through the ranks.

After I had been at Falconaire a few weeks he called me downtown to his office for a review of our operation. One of his questions was, "What were your sales last month?" I gave him my airplane salesman's answer of, "About $68,000." Gerry said, "I think it was $68,123. 69." He then proceeded to pull a big ledger out of a desk drawer, opened it, ran his finger down a column of figures and said, "Yes. 69 cents." Keep in mind, that here I am running a small division of a major corporation with 25,000 employees (we had 15) and operations extending from Seattle to Buffalo and from Canada to Kansas and he had in mind my sales to the penny! I never went to another meeting with Gerry without briefing myself for two days beforehand. Gerry gave me a real education, which helped me immensely in later years as a professional airplane salesman.

During that same meeting he asked me to prepare a twelve-month Cash Flow forecast for Faconaire. I said I would. The only problem was that at that time in my career I had no idea of what a Cash Flow was. However, with the help of Jerry Treble, our Office Manager at Minnesota Airmotive, I quickly learned how to do one. That Cash Flow was updated every 30 days and included all our anticipated purchases from Cessna for the next 12 months. Gerry Smith would buck that report over to Ken Osterberg, our consultant. If Ken signed off on that report, it became my authority to spend as much as $75,000 for a Cessna 310, or whatever, as long as it was in that Cash Flow. My normal spending limit was $2,000, but if it was in that signed-off Cash Flow, then that was my authority. Today, that would be equivalent to $750,000. A lot of authority.

I've always been thankful for the lessons I was given in Minneapolis by John Bean on how to compare aircraft and by Gerry Smith on how to understand and crunch numbers and how to speak the money language of the people downtown. It is interesting to note that the two men who taught me the basics of our present business were both Vice Presidents in the grain milling business in Minneapolis. No doubt, all part of my Instructor Pilot's long-range plan for me.

Working with Cessna, at that time, was an experience. Their philosophy seemed to be to push aircraft out the factory door and into the distributors hands and left it up to the distributors to figure out how to get rid of them. By contrast, Commander and Beech treated their distributors like partners. What was good for the distributor was good for the factory. Their way to move more airplanes was to create more buyers in the field, then the distributors would order more planes from the factory. Two entirely different philosophies. I did not enjoy working with the Cessna factory people, but did enjoy working with my dealers. I had two excellent dealers and one weak one. The others were just average—being more interested in flying their airplanes than selling them.

Greg Nelson was my strongest dealer. He not only got me into the QB (Quiet Birdmen) organization of pilots, but also introduced me to Beefeaters Gibsons. He was quite a guy and, coincidentally, John Stuber's brother-in-law. He and his partner ran Ryan Aviation at Flying Cloud Airport just southwest of Minneapolis. My weakest dealer—and good friend—was Sterling Blumshein at St. Paul Downtown Airport. A neat person, but he could louse up a deal faster than anyone I ever met. At one of my dealer meetings, a well-known aviation writer in St. Paul stated, for all to hear, "Sterling, you are a disgrace to your race." But we all loved him anyway.

Cessna tended to hire young, inexperienced regional sales reps. The factory would pump them all up and send them out into the field to show the distributors (most of whom were highly experienced in our business) how to sell Cessna airplanes. I was never very popular with them because I rarely paid any attention to their amateur marketing suggestions.

I remember one very self-righteous rep who went out to dinner with Clarence Morgan and me at Charlies's in Minneapolis. Clarence was a highly experienced Commander Regional Manager and we were long-time good friends from Commander days. Over dinner Clarence was chastising himself for having forgotten to close his flight plan into Minneapolis that afternoon. The Cessna rep, very self-righteously, informed us that he never forgot to close a flight plan, because if something was a part of his check list he couldn't forget it. Clarence and I just looked at each other and, for once, kept our mouths shut.

The next morning the Cessna rep pre-flighted his brand new Cessna 310 demonstrator and climbed in to proceed on to the next distributor in Madison, Wisconsin. As he started up his engines my Chief of Maintenance grabbed my arm and yelled, "Don't you think he should take off his tow-bar?" I jumped in front of his plane and held up my hands, removed the tow-bar from his nose-wheel, opened the cabin door and threw the tow-bar into the rear seat and said, "This is for the SOB who never forgets anything" and slammed the door shut. Well, I must have really unnerved him, because he flew on to the next distributor where he landed on their gravel surfaced runway with the gear up. The gravel effectively totaled the 310 and that fellow never came back to visit us again.

I was always of the opinion that it paid to be friendly with your competitors. This was easy to do in Minnesota, because the people there are inherently friendly. While we were working on a sale we would fight hard to win, but when it was over we would sit down over a beer and in a very friendly manner discuss what we had done right or wrong. We even had an Air Fair where all four distributors had aircraft on display in the almost adjoining hangars of the Cessna and Beech distributors, who were both neighbors at Fleming Field in South St. Paul. The Cessna factory people definitely did not approve of our friendly relations with the other distributors. They didn't even approve of our corporate relationship with the Commander distributor. Cessna was probably the most difficult corporation that I ever had to do business with and we would soon come to a parting of the ways.

In 1962 Cessna introduced the Cessna 320 Skyknight—a supercharged version of their standard 310 light twin. The superchargers gave it the ability to fly at high altitudes. On one of my visits to the factory, Frank Martin, VP Marketing, gave me a preview briefing of this "new" aircraft that was to "open up a whole new market of customers with a plane that could fly over weather. It would double the potential market for light twins for Cessna."

My reaction to the idea was to ask Frank if he could visualize the President of some corporation sitting in the back seat of his airplane trying to smoke his cigar while wearing an oxygen mask. I also went on to make the unwelcome observation that rather than opening up a new market, the 320 would simply divide the present market into two parts. The western buyers opting for the altitude performance and the eastern buyers sticking with the normally aspirated 310. These comments were not warmly received. They were not part of the factory's school solution. It was also the beginning of the end between the factory and Falconaire.

Later that year the Skyknight was introduced with great fanfare and each distributor was told that he had to order one as a demonstrator. I advised our Regional Manager that I already had a one year inventory of unsold 310s sitting in my hangar and that I didn't think that my parent company would permit me to order another twin until I had sold at least one of my present twins. As soon as I could sell one of my present inventory 310s, I'd order my Skyknight. I had already briefed Gerry Smith on this potential situation and if we didn't order one, it might cost us our franchise. His reaction was, "Well let's find out, right now, whether we are running our company or Cessna."

Sure enough, in a few weeks the factory man came in and advised us they were withdrawing their franchise. On hindsight it is interesting to note that Skyknight sales never exceeded much more than one for each remaining distributorship (their demonstrator) while 310 sales averaged almost an equivalent decrease each year. 1968 was the last year of production for the SkyKnight.

Closing up Falconaire was the most difficult job I ever had to do. I not only put myself out of a job, but also had to lay off all 14 other employees. I know that I made the right business decision, but it was no fun putting the others out of their jobs. I have never had much respect for the Cessna factory since that time.

Atlantic Aviation

1963 TO 1970

I WENT BACK TO MINNESOTA AIRMOTIVE for a short time, but wasn't really needed there any more. I had flown copilot for Jim Grogan, Chief Pilot for Pillsbury Mills, a couple of times in their Gulfstream I. Jim suggested that I contact his friend Don Redpath at Atlantic Aviation in Wilmington, DE. They sold Gulfstream, deHavelland 125 and Beech aircraft. Maybe Atlantic could use someone with my sales background.

I wrote to Don and he advised me that he didn't need anyone in Gulfstream or 125 sales, but they did need a Beech salesman at their Teterboro operation. Right across the street from where I had left to go back into the Air Force 15 years earlier. So, in 1963 Martha, our two girls, their two dogs and I were on our way back to New Jersey. I was soon selling Twin Beechs and Queen Airs in the Northeast area.

In 1965 Bill Crawford, our Sales Manager, called me to his office and said, "You are the only one here who has ever sold a pressurized aircraft. How would you like to go out to Wichita with Bill Watt (then our Chief Pilot) and bring back our new turboprop King Air demonstrator (s/n 6)?" This was the first King Air to leave the factory that was not a factory owned King Air. I guess that we got the first one, because New York was the prime market for the airplane and Atlantic was their top distributor. For me this became a license to steal. I liked the aircraft and its concept and for the next five years was heavily involved with the sale of turboprops.

Beech was funny at that time, because they were worried about selling 48 King Airs that first year. We kept telling them, "Just keep pumping them out. They will sell." I believe they got orders for 90 that first year and they are still selling them. I believe about 5,600 in one form or another, so far.

Bill Watt specked out that first demonstrator with ho-hum ARC avionics. Later, when it came time to order its replacement, with the help of Bob Prewitt and his guys at Collins Radio, we put on a dog and pony show and convinced our top management to equip the new demonstrator with a full Category II Collins Integrated Flight System and autopilot. This was top of the line avionics for a business aircraft. From that point on we only sold one King Air without that kind of first class radios installed.

We were then able to go in to a General Electric Company or an FMC Corporation and our small turboprop demonstrator was equipped just like their Gulfstream, Falcon or Sabreliner. We were speaking their language going in and at the same time increasing our gross dollar sales about 15% without increasing our unit sales. Soon the factory was equipping their demonstrators the same way. Incidentally, I was well treated by Collins Radio people in Cedar Rapids. Poor Ken Weiss was selling turboprop Merlins against us at this time and his demonstrators only had small aircraft radios installed. His boss, George Buchner, was more concerned about keeping the total price down than he was about image. Ken could not project the same professional image that we did with our Collins equipped demonstrator.

Many aircraft salesmen have this concern about "pricing themselves out of the market. It was my experience that if a prospect had X number of dollars to spend on an airplane, he would gladly spend X plus 15% without batting an eye to get something he wanted. In the early days of the King Air program, the factory people were concerned about its $400,000 price tag when their earlier top-of-the-line airplane sold for $200,000. However, the factory marketers quickly learned that if a company was comfortable spending $400,000 for a plane, then spending $450,000 was no problem just as long as it got them something that they wanted. George Buchner (head of Merlin sales) never understood this basic marketing fact and, when I worked for him a few years later in Sabreliner sales, we had a real donnybrook on this same subject.

One of my favorite King Air sales was to Sprague Electric in North Adams, MA. They owned two re-engined Twin Bonanzas from Ed Swearengin. They were looking for replacement aircraft and had a short-term lease on a Jet Commander to try out in their operations. The big problem for the Jet Commander was that Sprague operated out of North Adams, which was too small for the jet. So they kept it over at Albany, NY and hopped over there in their Twin Bonanza each time they wanted to use the jet. One day I was talking to Bob Sprague—executive in charge of their flight department—and he was all excited telling me about their recent "fast" trip to Dayton, OH. I listened to him for a bit and then deflated him by saying, "Bob, if you had used my "slow" King Air on that trip, you would have beaten the jet by 15 or 20 minutes. We would have departed right from North Adams, by-passed Albany and been in Dayton much sooner. And we would not have had to change airplanes."

Bob was not pleased with my comment, because he had his heart set on flying a jet. To make a long story short, cooler heads prevailed and I ended up selling Sprague Electric two matched King Airs with dual Collins Integrated Flight Systems. This presented a small problem for Beech, because Sprague wanted all avionics interchangeable between the two aircraft. This was also their first multiple King Air sale. Beech was so used to customizing each aircraft that they had problems making two exactly alike. Their delivery was also late because of a vendor supply problem and Bob Sprague really got on my back about that until we discovered that the vendor was Sprague Electric. Those two King

Airs did an excellent job for Sprague—out of North Adams and not Albany.

During one of my early visits to North Adams I was flying a Queen Air demonstrator. As I was getting ready to depart a pilot was there from our hangar at Teterboro Airport in his 680 Commander. There was the usual joshing back and forth between Beech and Commander drivers and the upshot was that I was challenged to a race back to Teterboro. We both taxied out together and I graciously allowed him to take off ahead of me, but not by much. I quickly caught up with him on the climb-out and flew formation with him on his left wing. After a couple of minutes of no effort flying on his left wing, I finally fire-walled the Queen Air and proceeded to pass him by. As I waved to him, he kind of playfully nudged his Commander towards my plane and I took up a heading straight to Teterboro. On arriving at TEB I asked for a straight in approach, because I didn't want that Commander driver to slip in ahead of me in the traffic pattern. As I turned off the runway I looked back and saw no Commander on the final approach. I taxied to the Atlantic Hangar ramp, parked my Queen Air, got out and still couldn't see him. After a couple of minutes went by I finally saw him coming in with his left engine feathered. His playful nudge as I passed him was caused by his losing his left engine just as I passed him. Of course I claimed that he just did that to have an excuse for losing the race.

Bill Blakemore was the General Manager of Atlantic's Teterboro operation and a really nice guy. All the top brass at Atlantic's Wilmington headquarters thought the sun rose and set at Bill's command. Anything Bill said about marketing was law. Well, Bill was a good aircraft salesman, but he was not perfect. Ronson Corporation (cigarette lighters) was a "house" account and handled by Bill. At one point, Mr. Aronson (owner of Ronson Corporation) and Alex Yankaskas (his pilot) got interested in a new Queen Air. I helped Bill crunch the numbers for the sale and was promised half the commission. When we were all set, Blakemore, Bill Patrick (then Office Manager at Teterboro) and I drove to the Ronson plant to finalize the deal.

I don't remember the details now, but Blakemore blew the deal and we did not finalize the sale. Several months went by and I knew that Alex was a Collins man and liked gadgets. Collins had just introduced their FD-108 Flight Director and, for once, I knew something about Collins equipment before Alex did. I arranged for Alex to fly the Flight Director in one of Collins demonstrators. Alex loved it and sold Mr. Aronson the idea that they should have one installed in a new Queen Air. Yankaskas talked Mr. Aronson into the idea and the next thing you knew we had an order for a new Queen Air with an FD-108 installed. Blakemore was good about it and I got the whole commission and Ronson became one of my accounts.

In addition to being our General Manager, Blakemore was a Senior Captain on TWA's European runs. TWA finally gave him an ultimatum to pick one career or the other and Bill elected to go full time with TWA. He left us with an archaic sales commission system that actually encouraged the salesman to cheat the company. No one ever did, but the incentive was there. This bothered Tom Reilly and myself, so over lunch hours and other odd times we developed a whole new proposed incentive plan for our salesmen. We found nothing worth salvaging in the old plan, so started with a clean sheet of paper. The incentive in our plan was to make more profit on the sale. After we had polished it up we took it to Bill Patrick (now our General Manager).

He looked through our plan and then laughed at us, asking what did we know about incentive plans. I told him that it had been part of my business for several years when I had been a Factory Regional Manager. We got no place with our plan and I don't like being laughed at when I'm being serious. I realized that it was time for me to move on to another company. I quietly started to look around, but I didn't want to move my family and I didn't want to move sideways in my profession. In the meantime, I continued to sell King Airs and continued to look around.

Business Jets

1970 TO 1984

IT IS EASY TO IMAGINE MY PLEASURE to receive a phone call in April 1970 from Don Redpath, who had been originally responsible for my coming to Atlantic. He had left Atlantic several months earlier, and was running the AiResearch facility at Mac Arthur Airport on Long Island where they were doing large aircraft maintenance, engine overhauls and aircraft completions. It seemed that AiResearch and Pan Am Business Jets had just signed an agreement to jointly market the Falcon business jet. Would I be interested in joining them and sell Falcons in the northeast? I thought that the Falcon was the best looking business jet out there and jumped at the opportunity. I also had worked with AiResearch's top executives in Los Angeles, while I had been with Aero Commander, and had liked the way they did business.

H.L. Richardson was the president of AiResearch and Landis Carr was in charge of all marketing arms of AiResearch. Merlin sales were headed by George Buchner and Falcon sales were headed by Don Payton. Don would be my immediate boss and made his headquarters in the Chicago area. Don was a very well organized and a very experienced marketing man. He knew about selling large aircraft and asked for only a minimum of reporting paperwork. If asked he would help a salesman, but, unlike Finn Hedlund—his counterpart at Pan Am—would never try to move in and take over a salesman's deal. Don always relied on his salesmen while Finn often felt he could handle the sale better than the salesman.

Don and Finn divided the country into five regions with one Pan Am and one AiResearch salesman in each region. Four Pan Am salesmen were to be based with AiResearch at their various facilities around the country and I was to be the token AiResearcher based with Pan Am at Teterboro. Don and Finn came up with the best technique I've ever seen for getting two salesmen to work together in the same region. It was really quite simple—no matter which one closed the sale, they both would get paid a full commission. It worked like a champ. In the northeast region my Pan Am partner was Pat Healy.

When I returned from my indoctrination tour of the Dassault Falcon plants in France I found on my desk a list of all the owners and likely prospects for Falcon 20 aircraft in the northeast region. I had never had that happen to me before, but it was an indication of the way Don Payton had things organized. Pat Healy had a copy of that list and he and I sat down with it and decided which of us had the best reason to work each account. We didn't care which one of us got to work the account, but we did want the one on it that had the best chance to close the sale. If a sale was made, we both got our commission. As a rule salesmen do not work well together, but this system solved the problem beautifully. Pat knew some people in the northeast that I didn't and I knew some that he didn't. Those that we both knew or did not know, we arbitrarily divided between us so that we had equal workloads. It was an excellent plan and really encouraged us to work together to close a sale

Shortly after I moved in with Pan Am Business Jets and began to try to sell Falcons, a young aeronautical engineer joined Pan Am as their Sales Engineer. His name was Bill de Decker and, because his office wasn't quite finished, shared my office for a short period of time. Bill and I both wanted a good, reliable set of relative costs for business jets, but couldn't find anything that was useful. For example, we went to the NBAA (National Business Aviation Association) and got 25 cost reports for the Sabre 40. Of those 25 reports, five showed Block Speeds faster than the Max Cruise Speed of the plane. One was even faster than the Red Line Speed (Never Exceed Speed) of the Sabre. Not much credibility there!

This caused me to make the remark to Bill that we could construct a set of numbers that would be more meaningful than anything we had found to date. Bill agreed and I laid out the ground rules and format. Bill calculated the block speeds and fuel burns and crunched the numbers. Thus began the long association, now known as Conklin & de Decker.

1970 was an awful year to sell business jets. Nobody was selling anything. Pan Am had about 40 green (no paint, interior or avionics installed) Falcon 20s in storage all around the country. I finally broke the log-jam with a sale to Butch Savin, Chairman of Savin Construction Company in Connecticut. I had sold Butch his King Air and we were on a first name basis. When I went to Chuck Fleming, President of Pan Am Business Jets, to set up a demo flight for Butch in one of our demonstrators, Chuck looked up Savin Construction Company and learned that it was only a small $6,000,000 a year company. He told me that they were too small to afford a Falcon. What he didn't know was that Butch had about seven of these small companies. Chuck very reluctantly let me run the demo—mostly, I guess, because we hadn't sold anything in so long a time.

The demo trip was to his horseracing farm near Ocala, FL. He liked the airplane and agreed to buy one of our inventory aircraft. I pulled out one of Pan Am's Purchase Contracts in its 2 1/2 inch three ring binder. Butch took one look at this imposing document and said, "You don't expect me to read that thing, do you?" I told him that most of it was just window dressing and that I would show him the important pages. Butch also wanted to make some minor changes to the deal, so I took the last page out of the binder, turned the page over, handed him my pen and told him to write out what he wanted. He gave me a horrified look and said, "Have you ever seen my handwriting?" After seeing a sample I agreed that if he dictated, I would write.

When we got finished I had a one page, hand written contract for a new Falcon signed by Butch. The next morning I walked into Chuck Fleming's office and handed him the one page contract. Chuck almost had a fit. It just wasn't the way Pan Am did business. I asked Chuck if it was a legal document and did he want to sell an airplane. To me it was that simple. Chuck worried about it for two days and finally signed Butch's order. For a long time a photocopy of that contract hung on my office wall.

An amusing side-light to this story was that while Butch and I were flying around Florida in our Falcon, the Sabre salesman was in Hartford, CT with the *President* of Savin Construction *knowing* that he was about to sell a Sabreliner. What he didn't know was that the President of Savin Construction was Butch's son and only Dad made the real decisions. Later, when I went with Sabreliner, that Sabre salesman never spoke to me except for matters of pure business. He never forgave me for stealing his sure-sale away from him. I just knew the prospect better than he did.

Back in that period of time AiResearch had a company policy that we could not spend more than $12.00 per person on entertainment. I had just started serious talks with Mr. Ridgeway, Chairman of Crum & Forster Insurance Company, about a Falcon 20. He told me that Bill Moore had just arrived in New York from California and was staying at the Hotel Pierre right near Central Park. Bill was to become their new Chief Pilot and we should both come to Mr. Ridgeway's office the next morning. Bill and I had known each other fairly well when we both flew out of Oakland, CA when I had been with Commander. I called Bill and arranged to take him and his wife out to dinner that night.

I don't like New York and rarely went there socially. On my way to the Hotel Pierre I was wracking my brain trying to figure out where I could take the Moores out to dinner. I met them in the lobby and gingerly asked them if there was anyplace in particular that they would like to go to for dinner. Bill said that the hotel had a good dining room so why not eat right there. With great relief I agreed to the suggestion. We didn't have anything real elaborate, but, being the Hotel Pierre, we ran up a tab significantly larger than allowed by the company policy. The bill came to $78.00 and that was what went into my weekly Expense Report.

A few days went by and I suddenly had an agitated phone call from Don Payton, my boss in Chicago. His first question was, "Are you trying to get me fired?" I said I didn't think so, but why? He said, "Your expense account for dinner is way over company policy." I told Don that I knew that, but that is what I spent. Don told me to bury the difference in other places in my expense report. I told Don that I don't do business that way. I spent $78.00 for dinner and they could either pay me or not. They didn't and I swallowed the $42.00 difference.

A couple of years went by and I was now working for Falcon. One day I had a call from Don who told me that he was in New York on a business trip and would Martha and I care to join him for dinner. I indicated that we would be delighted to join him. I learned that he was staying at the Hotel Pierre and did I know where it was located. I assured him that I did. We met Don in the lobby and I suggested that we have dinner right there in the hotel dining room. We went in and sat down. The waiter handed us our menus. I turned to Martha and said, "Don't pay any attention to anything on the left side of the page, but go down the right side and pick the most expensive items you can find. About this time the light went on in Don's head and he said, "Uh oh! It was right here, wasn't it?" I said, "Not only right here, but at this very table." Don howled and I got my $42.00 back in spades.

1970 was a terrible year for selling business jets. There were only five Falcons sold during the twelve months that AiResearch sold Falcons with Pan Am. We sold four and Pan Am sold one. At the end of the year Pan Am decided that they didn't need two large fish in that little pond, so they did not renew our agreement. So, once again I was an unemployed airplane salesman.

In looking around for employment, I went to the Beechcraft factory. They were in the process of taking over the marketing of the Hawker 125 business jet. We agreed to agree, but Beech asked me to hold off for a couple of weeks while they settled their contract disagreements with Atlantic Aviation. Beech didn't want my former association with Atlantic to create any undue problems. This was OK with me and ultimately Beech cancelled their contract with Atlantic.

With a few days to kill on my hands, I suggested to Beech that I go down to Bethany, Oklahoma to look over Rockwell's then brand new Sabre 75. Rockwell owned both Sabreliner in Los Angeles and Commander in Bethany and they had sent the first Model 75 to Bethany for completion. This new model would be a direct competitor to the Hawker 125. Beech knew that I knew my way around the Commander plant and thought it was a great idea. I should mention here that after a year of poor aircraft sales, morale at Beech was very low.

So, off I went to Bethany to check out the new Sabre. When I walked into the headquarters of the General Aviation Division of Rockwell at Bethany you could feel their high morale. As I told someone at the time, "They were too dumb to know that they were out of business." Dick Robinson was their President and I had known him when he was our Regional Manager for Cessna when I was in Minnesota. On one of his trips to Falconaire I had even thrown him out of my office. When Dick learned that I was in the plant, he invited me into his office for a chat.

Dick really did a sales job on me and, much to my surprise, persuaded me to come with Rockwell and sell Sabres in the northeast. He had heard about my sale of the Falcon to Savin Construction Company. During the course of our conversation, Dick asked me, "Now I want a straight answer. Just how many Falcons did you sell last year?" I said, "Dick, I like to say that I sold 60% of all the Falcons sold last year. It sounds much more impressive than saying three." Dick howled and I suspect it was what got me the job offer.

I really had some strong misgivings about going with Sabre. I really did not approve of the way Dick ran his business. He was a driver, not a leader. But for the two years that I worked for him, he never gave me any grief. Everyone in the Sabre Division, except me, was terrified of him. Dick knew that I was not afraid of him and knew that he could call me and get a straight answer, even though it might not be one that he wanted to hear. The result was that we got along fine. One thing we agreed on was to establish a joint Sabreliner/Aero Commander sales office at Westchester County Airport in White Plains, NY. If I couldn't upgrade someone into a jet, I'd call in the turboprop Commander salesman and Vice versa. It worked very well.

At one time, when we hadn't sold a Sabre in months, I got Hershey Foods sold on a Sabre 40A. There was a small problem. George Buchner, formerly with AiResearch was now VP Marketing for Sabreliner and was still hung up on selling price. He had packaged the Sabre 40A, as a price leader, with inexpensive King Avionics to get the selling price down to $995,000. You could choose from four different colors and almost no options. However Hershey wanted Collins airline type radios. George wouldn't budge on the avionics, because it would take the selling price over $1,000,000. I could not convince him that Hershey would pay the difference. Just tell me what it would add to the cost.

I finally called Dick Robinson on the telephone, explained the problem and asked if he wanted to sell a Sabre or not. Hershey wanted Collins equipment. Needless to say I got the selling price of a Collins equipped Sabre. I believe that this limited view of marketing is what shortly cost George his job at Sabreliner. That sale to Hershey broke the log-jam at Sabreliner and the rest of the year's sales went reasonably well.

It is interesting to note that the current edition of *The Aircraft Bluebook Price Guide* shows that, in 1972, the Factory New List Price for an average equipped Sabre 40A was $1,200,000. This is quite a bit more than the Standard List of $995,000. Apparently no one wanted George's inexpensive King avionics package.

One of the more interesting threads in the pattern of my adventures selling corporate aircraft has been my involvement with IBM going back for 46 years. I first became acquainted with Chuck McKinnon, their first Director of IBM Flight Operations when he came to pick up their Aero Commander at the factory in Bethany, OK. Then in April, 1973 we delivered a personal Sabre to Tom Watson, Chairman of IBM. Tom Reilly actually made the sale to Tom, but for some reason I was asked to handle the delivery in St. Louis. I was his host in St. Louis during the last few days of his Ground School and aircraft checkout.

My birthday occurred on Tom's last day of checkout and we celebrated it and his new jet rating at dinner that night. He was kind enough to give me an IBM tie for my birthday and hoped I wouldn't find it too conservative. We also talked about my wife's adventures going back to college in her early fifties and all-in-all had a most enjoyable evening. There will be more about this evening almost one year later, shortly after I joined the Business Jets Division of Pan Am.

The next day, while Tom and I handled the paper work, Tom's wife, Olive, supervised the transfer of their personal gear and ski equipment from their King Air to their new Sabre. We took the King Air in trade. We toted up all the loose ends and I told Tom what the cash difference was—about $900,000. I was a little surprised when he reached into his jacket pocket and pulled out a small folding checkbook. He snapped out a check and wrote a personal check for the full amount. We traded papers. I watched him climb into his new Sabre, taxi out, take off and head in the general direction of Aspen. As the landing gear retracted and the plane disappeared into the distance, I suddenly had a horrible thought. I had just taken a personal check for $900,000! Definitely not company policy, but I need not have worried. The check was good.

In the middle of 1973 we had a big marketing meeting at Rockwell's headquarters in Los Angeles. One of the items on the agenda was what airplane we should develop next. We already had a small Sabre 40A, a stretched Sabre 60 and a medium sized

Sabre 75A. We rapidly discarded the idea of an inexpensive jet like Cessna's successful Citation. First, Rockwell didn't know how to build an inexpensive jet and there was already too much competition in that segment of the market.

Several years earlier, Don Payton had convinced me of the concept that a long range, over water business jet should have three engines. This would give the passenger in a business jet the same safety factor given to a passenger on a commercial airliner, which was required to have more than two engines on long over water flights. Two was too few, four was too expensive to operate and that left three as the optimum choice. I had become a strong believer in the concept, so I brought up the idea in our marketing meeting. The engineers agreed that the Sabre 75 could be stretched and grown to produce a three-engine Sabre with 3,000 nautical mile range and could sell for $3,000,000. 3-3-3 made a nice marketing package and with no immediate competition. We turned to our engineers and asked, "How much to develop this new model plane?" They got out their slide-rules, made some quick calculations and told us it would take $52,000,000.

Wayne Smiley, the new VP Marketing, took the proposal to Mr. Anderson, President of Rockwell, for approval. His response was, "You haven't made a damn dimes profit on any Sabre sold to date. Why should I approve $52,000,000 to have you loose more money?" "Thus ended, I thought, my dream of a three engine intercontinental business jet.

A couple of months went by, and one day I had a call from my old friend Finn Hedlund at Falcon Jet. He wanted to know if I would be interested in coming to work for Falcon. My response was, "That I had a good job at Rockwell. Why should I change?" His reply was to offer me the job of National Sales Manager and to also mention that Dassault (the manufacturer) was planning to build an intercontinental version of the medium sized Falcon 20. Dassault had presented two versions, one with two engines and one with three engines. The factory liked the two-engine version, but Finn inclined toward the one with three engines. That did it.

Here was the good possibility of my dream of an intercontinental business jet, so I quickly resigned from Rockwell and joined my old friends at Falcon Jet. And besides I lived in North Jersey and wouldn't have to commute to White Plains every day. We quickly found that Bill de Decker also believed in the three-engine concept. So, we went to work and sold Dassault on the concept of three engines. Thus was born the Falcon 50.

As originally conceived, Dassault planned to remove the Falcon 20's two-engine tail and replace it with a three-engine tail. Basically this was a pretty simple engineering change. When engineering took their proposal in to Marcel Dassault for approval, he looked at it carefully and finally said, "Gentlemen, we have never built a three engine aircraft and it looks like fun. But let's do it right. Put on our new wing." The old man ran the company and we got a whole new aircraft. What a change from the "committees for committees" approach at Rockwell where no one wanted to make a decision that might be wrong. But to Marcel Dassault the idea of three engines just felt right and he made the decision.

Dassault has always been a leader in utilizing new technology and, at that point, was really into the development of their CATIA (Computer Aided Design) program (now used by Boeing and most of the other manufacturers). We got a new super critical wing, similar to the one on the then new Falcon 10, and a new light-weight fuselage structure. The only part of the airframe that was the same as the original Falcon 20 was the cockpit and nose. All these changes cost us 18 months of time, but gave Dassault an aircraft that has been in production for 21 years and is still the most versatile business jet out there. I like to think of the Falcon 50 as "My baby." I'm certain that Dassault is glad they listened to Finn, Bill and myself back in 1974.

It is always interesting to look back and see the interweaving of the threads that make up the patterns of our lives. In the spring of 1974 I went to work as the National Sales Manager of the Business Jets Division of Pan Am selling Falcons. A few weeks after I came aboard I was in a meeting with Chuck Fleming, our

President and Finn Hedlund, our VP of Marketing. My secretary stuck her head in the door to tell me that Mr. Watson wanted to talk to me. Naturally I took the call. Chuck Fleming's ears promptly perked up, because Tom Watson was on Pan Am's Board of Directors. When I picked up the phone, Tom's first remark was, "Don't you have a birthday coming up soon?" I said, "Yes, in about two weeks." He then went on to inquire how Martha was doing in college and I updated him on her activities. Then he went on to ask some technical questions about our new Falcon 10 and I briefed him. Then I went back to my meeting. Chuck was all excited and asked, "What did he want? What did he want?" Suddenly, I become Joe Cool and stated that he wanted to check on my birthday, which is in about two weeks." "Yes, yes, but then what did he want?" My Joe Cool answer was that he wanted to know how Martha was doing in College. From that point on, anything dealing with IBM was handed off to Pan Am's new National Sales Manager.

In July, 1975 I had an urgent call from Ed Sowa, the current Director of IBM Flight Operations. They had just lost one of their Gulfstreams in a training accident at Savannah. To replace it they planned to pull in their other Gulfstream from their Paris operation and replace it with two Falcon 20E models. How quickly could we deliver two? I told him that we had one green one in inventory and I thought Dassault might have one in France. Ed told me that if we could deliver right away, we had just sold two Falcon 20s.

Dassault did have one and I went in to tell Chuck Fleming the good news. His first reaction was to ask if we had a deposit and I said no. He then asked if we had a signed purchase order, and once again I said no. Chuck then said, "You expect me to order a $2,000,000 airplane from Dassault with no paperwork?" I said, "Only if you want to sell two falcon 20s. It will take six weeks for IBM to process their paperwork and this is an emergency." The deal went through without a hitch. Chuck always hated anything that didn't follow the Pan Am procedures.

M. Maisonrouge, President of IBM France wanted the French built Falcons in Europe. George Zieres, our Falcon Completions Manager, Hientz Wentzel, our Avionics Manager and I went to Paris to work with Francois Chavatte, IBM's Aviation Manager in Paris and M. Maisonrouge to work out the final details for completing their two Falcons. We had a meeting scheduled at Maisonrouge's office the morning after we arrived.

Heintz Wenzel was an interesting individual. Although now an American citizen, during WW II he had flown FW 190 fighters in the Luftwaffe. At dinner he educated George and myself about how WW II had really gotten started. It was considerably different from the way George and I had learned.

In the morning, at the last minute, Heintz had to rush out to the airport to get some final measurements for the avionics installation, while George and I went to M. Maisonrouge's office. We knew that M. Maisonrouge liked Autumn colors, so had prepared two different color boards, in Autumn colors, with fabric samples to illustrate the kind of interiors we could supply. You might imagine our genuine surprise to discover that one of our boards exactly matched his office decor. He looked at them both and indicated that he couldn't make up his mind between them. Finally, he said, "We are getting two aircraft. Why don't we do one of each. Actually I don't care what the color is, just as long as it isn't that damned Wehrmacht Green!" At this point I noted the Resistance ribbon in his lapel button-hole. George and I quickly looked at each other and almost died. By pure chance we sent that slightly unreconstructed Nazi out to the airport instead of bringing him to M. Maisonrouge's office. If we had, we probably would have blown a two airplane deal. My Instructor Pilot was sure with me on that day.

Early on in my time with Falcon Jet, we had a visit from a Democratic Congressman from Staten Island. This was during the Nixon era. During the course of his visit he asked us what we thought of the Coast Guard recently giving a Sole Source (no bids) Procurement Contract to Rockwell International for Sabre 75s.

We told him we didn't like it because all the CG ever asked from us was information about our small Falcon 10, then gave Rockwell a contract for medium jets. We added that we believed our Falcon 20 was superior to the Sabre in all five of the areas that the CG felt were important.

It seemed that the congressman was on the CG Oversight Committee. He asked if we would be willing to come to Washington and testify to his committee on this subject, because they couldn't get any of the other manufacturers to testify. Suddenly the yellow flag of caution went up and we asked why no one else would testify. It seemed that each had a plane in the middle of certification or some other similar situation and they had been cautioned not to talk. Being a small manufacturer, and also French, they had not bothered with us. We told him we would get back to him.

Bill and I huddled with Tim McCool, our Legal Counsel, and Chuck Fleming, our President. The consensus was that we should go to Washington and testify to the CG Committee. However, Chuck first wanted to know how much this would cost. We estimated that it would take $75,000 to do a proper presentation. Then he wanted to know what we thought the odds were that we could succeed in shooting Rockwell out of the saddle for this contract. We told him about 10%, because of Rockwell's long relationship with the government in military aircraft sales. Then he wanted to know what the odds were of our getting the contract if we were successful in getting the contract reopened for competitive bidding. Our estimate was zero, because we were a French company and the US Government didn't normally purchase foreign built aircraft. Chuck's response was, "With those kind of odds you want me to give you $75,000?" We told him that we believed someone had to do it.

We did not get our $75,000 for a proper presentation. So Bill, Tim—who knew his way around in the Washington bureaucracy— a young girl artist from Greenwich Village and I put in 18 hour days for about 10 days to put together our dog and pony show.

We scronged any needed funds from advertising budgets or any other source we could find. It was probably the single most fun project I have ever worked on.

I knew both the Sabre and the Falcon intimately, so did the basic comparisons. Bill translated my stuff into effective charts and graphs and our little artist made them into colorful posters. Tim McCool, our Legal Counsel, steered us through the potential pitfalls of Washington. Bill did the actual presentation to the Coast Guard Committee. Well, it all worked and the CG was directed to reopen the contract for competitive bidding. We had done it! Now, all of a sudden, our project became Chuck Fleming's project.

Soon the CG sent out specifications for the plane they wanted. In looking through the spec one item jumped out at me and really caught my attention. The pilot seats had to have 45 degree beveled inside corners for easy access for the pilots. This was a standard option on all Sabres because of its relatively narrow fuselage and not needed in a Falcon or a Hawker. I then went through the spec with a fine toothed comb and discovered that about one third was, word for word, right out of the standard published spec for a Sabre 75. Rockwell had helped the CG write their spec. Bill and I promptly wrote a White Paper on the subject and sent it off to Washington.

Eventually we got our chance to submit our bid to the CG. Chuck Fleming took it upon himself to handle this chore. His whole approach to submitting our bid was based on the assumption that Rockwell was the only other real competitor. The afternoon before the bids were to be submitted I happened to be talking to a friend at Sabreliner and naturally the subject of the next day's bid submissions came up. He mentioned that Rockwell wasn't even going to bother to submit a bid. I promptly called Chuck in Washington and advised him of this news, but he didn't believe it. Falcon submitted its bid as planned. Rockwell did not submit a bid and this cost Falcon a bundle of money for an unnecessarily low bid. But we did get the contract for the CG HU-25s that are still seeing service today.

Dassault had started to deliver the small Falcon 10 shortly before I came aboard. In those days the competition among the small jets was pretty intense, especially between Lear and Falcon. At one point Citation was having a tough time selling against their two high performing competitors. So, they started an advertising campaign that pushed their low operating costs (per hour) against the much more "expensive" (per hour) high performance Lear 35 and Falcon 10.

When dealing with relatively slow piston powered aircraft, Cost per Hour was a reasonable way to measure relative costs—something Cessna had been doing for decades before 1974. However, when I first became involved with turboprop powered aircraft in 1965 I learned that the only valid way to compare costs was by the mile rather than by the hour. The reason being that the turbine powered twin covers 20% more miles in one hour than the equivalent piston aircraft. I knew that the Falcon 10's cost per mile was much lower than the Citation (61 cents per mile to their 66 cents per mile), because we traveled 100 miles further in one hour than the Citation. So I gave my numbers to Tom Grant, our advertising man, and Falcon ran some ads pushing our lower costs compared to the Citation and, in addition, we had speed.

All went well for a couple of weeks, until we got a strongly worded letter from Cessna's Legal Counsel telling us to cease and desist from our misleading advertising. Tom Grant showed me the letter and I became a little nervous. I rechecked my calculations, which were OK, and sent them to Cessna and asked them to show us where we were wrong. They never responded, but very shortly Cessna stopped their cost advertising against the high performance jets and turned it around against the turboprops. This was a fun game and another payoff from the basic training my Instructor Pilot had arranged for me back in Minnesota.

In September 1980 my Instructor Pilot once again showed me that He was still in charge. My wife Martha and a couple of her friends decided to take up Racket Ball for exercise. She knew that I had always enjoyed Hand Ball, while we were in the Air Force, and she had always liked Tennis and believed we could both have fun playing Racket Ball. I agreed. A short time later she took her annual physical and mentioned playing Racket Ball to our family Doctor. Steve told Martha that he strongly recommended that she take a Stress Test and if I was to play, it was mandatory.

I was soon set up for a Stress Test. After they had me all wired up for the test, the Doctor came into the room, took one look at the gauges and didn't even bother putting me on the treadmill. He scheduled me for the first available slot for By-Pass surgery at Roosevelt Hospital in New York City. I had not had any symptoms of a heart problem up to that time. When they did discover my problem, there was no time for delay. I got the first available space at Roosevelt. My IP was certainly with me at that time and I thank him for getting Martha interested in Racket Ball.

After my By-Pass surgery, Dr. Green sent me home, but had me on a very short leash for six weeks. Martha and I had been becoming more and more involved with the Community of Jesus on Cape Cod and they had planned a weekend Family Retreat just about the time my six weeks of house arrest were up. We were anxious to attend that retreat and at the last minute Dr. Green gave me an OK to go. The folks at the Community were thoughtful enough to assign us to stay in room #3 in the Bethany Retreat House, so that I wouldn't have to run around so much. Room #3 also has a small alter in it. It was here that I had a life changing experience.

Martha had been coming to the Community for several years and I knew that she would like to move there. But as a successful airplane salesman in the New York area the whole idea could not have been further from my mind. Saturday afternoon was a silent time in the retreat and Martha and I were in room #3 observing that silent time. Suddenly, and in a loud and clear voice, I heard my Instructor Pilot talking to me and I was surprised at what He was telling me. I grabbed a piece of paper and scribbled a note to Martha. I wrote, "I think we are supposed to move here." That note is still in our Bible. Three months later we bought 1/2 of a house in the Community and I began a lot of weekend commuting between New York and Cape Cod.

In 1980 we started to deliver the first three-engine Falcon 50s. The first one to come to the US was a Dassault completed demonstrator. It was flown to the US by Dassault's Chief Falcon Test Pilot, Herve LaPrince Ringet. Herve was a very good-looking, charismatic bachelor with a great sense of humor. Herve was well known here in the business jet community and well liked by everyone.

During the development of the Falcon 50, there was much heated discussion about where to locate the lavatory in the aircraft. Dassault, championed by M. Valliere, the President of Dassault and former military aide to General Charles deGaulle, wanted to move the lavatory from the rear of the cabin forward to the cabin entry area. The idea was to better utilize the wasted space in the entry-way and free up more seating room in the passenger seating area. This was a good idea, except for two major problems. First was the very complicated arrangement of folding and interlocking doors between the cockpit and the lavatory and then between the lavatory and the cabin. The second problem was the psychological fact that, for some reason, women are reluctant to go forward to use a lavatory (especially when it adjoins the cockpit), but don't seem to object to going aft. I don't explain it, I just know it exists.

I can even remember sitting across the desk of M. Valliere vehemently debating this subject with him and, at one point even pounding my fist on his desk to try to make my point. Needless to say I lost the battle and the first few Falcon 50s were completed in France with forward lavs. With all this as background, we all waited breathlessly for Herve to bring over that first Falcon 50. Our President, Chuck Fleming, was very conservative, a teetotaler and very straight-laced. For this noteworthy occasion he had invited a number of dignitaries and members of the press.

Finally, Herve taxied up in front of our hangar with the left side and cabin door facing Chuck and his guests. The airstair door dropped open and there, standing in the doorway, was Herve waving to all the guests and Falcon employees. Then he hopped down to greet everyone and a startled gasp went up from us on the ground. Opposite the cabin entry door, on the paneled folding lavatory doors, Herve had hung a lightweight plastic replica of a urinal complete with plumbing. Chuck Fleming almost died, but the rest of us howled. Herve had given us the well-equipped forward lav. A Falcon first.

Shortly after the Falcon 50's started to arrive, Falcon Jet got a new President named Corky Meyer. About 10 days after coming on board, Corky called an after-work meeting for all the department managers. It started with a "happy hour" and then Corky stepped up to the podium with a highball glass in his hand. At that point we all realized we were under a new leadership and that a breath of fresh air had just blown in.

Shortly before Corky came aboard, I had been demoted to running the used aircraft sales department at Falcon. It was my punishment for standing up to top management over a couple of Falcon 50 sales contracts and telling them that I would testify for the customer over a couple of potential lawsuits. This was not a popular stand to take with top management. By assigning me to used aircraft sales it was assumed that I would resign and I actually was beginning to look around.

But then Corky came aboard and I happened to sit next to him at lunch one day at our facility in Little Rock, AR. He asked me some questions about our used aircraft sales department and talked about how he would like to make it grow. The more I listened to him the more I liked what I heard. I decided to stick with him and it was a good decision. I even agreed with him to get rid of The Used Aircraft Sales Department name and call it anything else. We promptly became The Pre-Owned Aircraft Department. We agreed on almost everything, whether it was about policy or about personnel. We not only enjoyed working together, but also became good friends.

Once again it is interesting to see my Instructor Pilot's hand in my life. When I got demoted into used aircraft sales it was a real blow to my ego and pride and I felt I had gotten a raw deal. On hindsight I realize that He was looking out for me once again. In 1980 the bottom dropped out of new aircraft sales and corporations purchased used aircraft instead. Our Pre-Owned sales never slowed down. At the time, I didn't know I was supposed to sell Pre-Owned Aircraft, but He sure did. He was in charge.

I stayed with Falcon Jet for four more years and the selling of pre-owned Falcons was very good to me. Bob Dandeneau came aboard as Director of Pre-Owned Aircraft Sales and we made a good team. Late in May 1984 I advised Bob that I intended to take an early retirement and start my own business up on Cape Cod. He got a funny look on his face and asked when I intended to leave. I said, "June first." Bob said, "That's the same day I was planning to leave. That would be kind of tacky if we both left the same day. Why don't you go ahead and take the first and I'll take the 31st." That was what we did. I started Al Conklin Associates (later called Conklin & de Decker Associates) and Bob started Peregrine Aviation and we've both been having a ball for the past 16 years.

Conklin & de Decker

1984 TO PRESENT

 OUR LITTLE COMPANY THAT WE STARTED on Cape Cod is a miracle in itself. About the time of my problems with the top management of my last employer, my wife and I became very involved with the Community of Jesus on Cape Cod. I tried all kinds of ways to find employment as an aircraft salesman in the Boston area. Every time I found a door of opportunity, it closed before I got there. At one time in my career I had been a top Beechcraft King Air turboprop salesman for Beech's biggest distributor. I was in control and when I went for a job interview at the factory store at Hanscom Field outside Boston I learned that I was "over qualified" and the door closed. My Instructor Pilot knew that that was not where I was supposed to be.

Shortly thereafter Martha and I spent a weekend at the Community of Jesus where I got some excellent counseling. It was suggested that I give up trying to control everything and turn the problem over to God—my Instructor Pilot. I went home with a significantly different attitude and tried to let Him have control. That was Sunday. On Tuesday I had a call from Don Harner who was then Manager of Flight Operations for Allied Automotive Sector (formerly Bendix Corporation) in Detroit.

Each Spring it was Don's custom to call me and ask for a copy of what I then called *Operating and Ownership Cost Analysis*. It was a compilation of relative operating costs for all business jets. I used the data to help me sell business jets and photocopied the report for anyone who wanted a copy. This was in early May of 1984 and at that time I was giving away about 200 copies of my report each year. Don was getting ready to do his annual budget update and wanted a copy of my latest costs. After we chatted for a few minutes he asked, "Are you thinking of retiring anytime soon?" My response was that I hadn't even thought about it and why? Don then said, "If you retire, where will I get my numbers each year? Why don't you publish your numbers? I'd be happy to buy them from you, because you save me so much time each year."

Well I thought that that was an interesting suggestion and went on about my business. About an hour later another customer said essentially the same thing and a light finally went on in my head. That night I talked with Martha about this seemingly crazy idea. We put a pencil to some numbers and both came to exactly the same conclusion that publishing my cost report was what we were supposed to do. It also meant that we could live on Cape Cod. A couple of close friends in the business agreed that we had a good idea and one week later I handed in my request for early

Bob Dandeneau helps Alan open gifts the night of his retirement party in May 1984. Jean Rosenvallon is with his back to the camera

retirement and one month later we published our first handbook entitled *The Aircraft Cost Evaluator.*

While all this was going on, the Community of Jesus had a small printing company, called Paraclete Press, doing in-house printing. About this time they decided to do outside printing and we became one of their first outside customers. They also had a spare office 10 by 10 feet square which Martha and I took over for our new little company, at that time called Al Conklin Associates. Suddenly all the doors that for two years had been closing on us, suddenly began to open and our little company took off and began to grow.

Martha and I figured that we needed 100 customers to survive that first year, along with Social Security and all. At the end of that first 12 months in business we had 200 customers and we were off and running. It started as a nice little Mom and Pop operation. It was all because we were trying to be obedient to God's will. Prior to 1984 no one had ever published a database similar to ours. We had no idea what would happen or really where we were going, but we both were convinced that this is what He wanted us to do. Why? I don't know, but we are having a great time doing it and we also get to live in His community here on the Cape. And I get to play airplanes every day. How fortunate can one be?

One year later, we agreed to publish a second handbook on the costs for turboprops. This was an easy jump for me because I was familiar with turboprops. It took a little more of my time, but expanded our customer base. All the time we were earning a reputation for integrity, even- handedness and reliability. One manufacturer said that our cost numbers "were the standard of the industry." These were nice words for an old airplane salesman to hear.

In 1988 I was pushed—fighting it all the way—into adding a third cost book for helicopters. I really wanted no part of doing this book for helicopters, because I knew nothing about helicopter operations. However, my customers insisted. So, in the summer of 1988 I took a crash course on helicopter operations and we added a third set of books to our collection. Of particular help with this project was the Textron Flight Department in Providence who are long-time friends in the fixed wing area and they operated a couple of helicopters. Textron also owns Bell Helicopter. Another big assist with this project, was provided by Vaughn Asque of Sikorski Helicopters in Hartford, CT. His biggest help was in suggesting, "The best person in the business to talk to about helicopter operating costs is Brandon Battles at Bell." Here again is evidence of the Lord's hand in all of this. Brandon has now been with our company about six years and is a partner in the company. More about this part of the story later.

In 1989 I realized that Martha and I had found a highly specialized, small, niche market with the databases we published. Being 69 years old, I started looking around for a younger partner to keep our company going. I found a young man in Florida who seemed to be a likely candidate. He was a very active Christian and his children attended Christian schools. Our kind of people. He was also a good sales engineer for an airframe manufacturer. Just the kind of person I was looking for. However, after we tried working on some projects together I realized that this was not a combination that would work.

First, he could never make a deadline for any of his projects. Then I discovered that he had taken a new job in Denver without ever telling me about what he was thinking. This is not a good way to promote trust, which is a must, in a good partnership. I broke off the relationship right away and started to look for someone else.

At the National Business Aviation Association convention that Fall came the opportunity I had been looking for. At the convention I ran into Bill de Decker who had helped develop the original operating cost database for jets twenty years earlier. I had laid out the format and ground rules for the original cost comparisons and Bill had crunched the numbers. He was now working for a large corporation and was running their publications division. He and I had stayed in touch over the years and were good friends. I told Bill that, "If you ever get tired of working for a big corporation and want to have some fun, you might like to consider buying me out and take over my business." He listened to me, nodded and went on his way.

Early in 1990 Bill called me from Texas and said, "OK, I'm ready." I said, "OK, except I'm not ready to retire. I'm having too much fun." At Bill's suggestion, he came up to Cape Cod for a weekend and we brainstormed ideas on how to make the little pond I had built for one fish, big enough for two.

One idea that I came up with was one that had been floating around in my mind for several months. It was for a binder full of aircraft comparisons—not costs, but performance and specifications information. One of the jet manufacturers that I had worked for had made up a few sets for us to study for a new model and its competitors. There were six pages of information with charts and graphs. Each page had a corresponding colored transparency and all were on the same set of scales. For instance, if you wanted to look at the cabin floor plan and cross section of one plane you simply took the transparency of one, laid it over the hard copy of the second plane and you had an instant visual comparison. It was a great sales tool, especially when talking with executives and other non-technical people.

My problem was that I had no graphics artist available that knew anything about airplanes. Also, printing on clear Mylar was a problem here on Cape Cod. From his experience in the publishing business, Bill could solve both problems. We also talked to the airframe manufacturer to see if they would mind if we took their idea and considerably expanded it. They said it sounded OK, but that they would like to look it over before we went to press. Incidentally, they liked what we had done and ordered two sets of the books. Today we have over 280 active subscribers to what we call *The Aircraft Comparators* and there are seven 2 1/2 inch binders to the complete set. So we were off and running. Our little pond was getting bigger.

Bill and I decided that we would work together informally that first year to make certain that this was what we both wanted to do.

Bill took over the helicopter side of the business and started bringing in consulting projects. I kept the fixed wing part moving and handled the administrative and production side of our company. All went smoothly and in 1990 we formalized our partner- ship and Bill started buying the majority of the company's stock. There were probably two major reasons why things went smoothly. First, was the simple fact that Fort Worth, TX is about 1700 miles from Cape Cod. We were not always looking over each other's shoulders. The other thing was that 20 years earlier we had worked together and at one point actually shared the same office. Each knew how the other worked. No doubt, all part of God's long range planning.

Bill's talents and mine have always complemented each other. What I was good at, Bill was weak in. What he did well, I didn't. We have never felt any competitiveness with each other. But it never ceased to amaze me how we always came to the same answer to a problem. Our boss, in the 1970's, would call each of us in, individually, and ask us the same question. I'd sniff the air, test the water, check the wind and come up with an answer of nine. Then he'd call Bill in and ask him the same question. Bill would start back with the Wright Brothers and factually develop his case and come to the same answer—nine. It never failed.

In 1991 Bill and I were both working with Jack Alcot and *Business & Commercial Aviation* magazine on a series of aviation management seminars around the country. One was in Chicago and over breakfast one morning I confessed to Bill that I was always jealous of his ability to analyze and prove his solution to a problem with facts and figures. Bill's response was that he was always jealous of me, because I never had to go through the process to arrive at the same answer. That is the way we have always worked together.

Our part of the BCA seminars involved Aircraft Analysis and Selection. We discovered that there was no good textbook on the subject. Over that same breakfast we came to the conclusion that the only real solution to this problem was to write one ourselves.

It took some time and a lot of doing, but in the Fall of 1998 we published our first textbook entitled *Aircraft Acquisition Planning* by Al Conklin and Bill de Decker. There are two more coming along behind it.

The story of those textbooks is interesting. It started out to be one book. Bill sketched out an outline for the book and we each took one part. Brandon Battles, being a Certified Public Accountant, took the accounting part, Bill took acquisition planning and I took financial management. We each started writing our own part of the book. Then Bill got a call from the General Services Administration in Washington asking us to write an aircraft cost accounting guide for the government agencies operating civil aircraft. Brandon took his part of the textbook and quickly developed the *Government Aircraft Cost Accounting Guide,* which is now the official Aircraft Cost Accounting Guide for all civilian government agencies.

They liked it so much that they asked Bill to write one on aircraft acquisition planning. He had been putting on seminars in Washington on this subject. Bill quickly finished up his section to our textbook. From a commercial point of view there was only one problem. It was written for bureaucrats in governmenteze. So, I took Bill's book and translated it into English and added a bunch of "war stories" to try to make a dull subject a little more interesting. We call this book *Aircraft Acquisition Planning.* So, instead of having one textbook, we will soon have three, thanks to being pushed by Uncle Sam.

Early in our partnership, Bill would bring in a consulting job. We'd take a look at the project and then divide the work into two parts. I'd take one part and Bill the other. Each of us had our own area of expertise and each could rely on the other to do a good job in the final report. Then we would combine the two sections into one report. It worked very well in helping to spread the workload. The consulting part of our business has been growing ever since.

One of the ideas I was working on when Bill joined the company was a simple chart listing the long term, big-ticket items of maintenance (that were not routine) on the various aircraft. I felt

The Conklins and the de Deckers in front of our Cape Cod office.

operators should be aware of these expenses in looking at the costs of different aircraft. Bill liked the idea in general, but said that if we were going to do it, let's do it right. Thus was born our computerized *Life Cycle Cost Analyzer* program. I continued to collect the data and Bill constructed the computer program on which to hang the various cost elements. It covers all costs for periods as long as twenty years. It answers such diverse questions as, buying new vs. used aircraft, and should we buy a recent model with high total time

Award Winners

As reported in ROTOR Magazine Alan Conklin and Bill de Decker were recipients of the HAI Excellence in Communications Award for 2000

vs. an older plane with low total time. Our regular databases only showed routine maintenance and could only be used to show the relative costs of operating different models of aircraft. Our LCCA program permits comparing two different serial numbers of the same model.

We were a couple of months into developing our LCCA program when the Coast Guard called and asked us if we could help them with a single large business jet purchase by developing a special life cycle cost program to go out with their Request For Proposal (RFP). We told them we were already working on such a program and that if we could have just a little time, we'd sell them our commercial version rather than designing a custom package just for this one contract The CG liked the idea and we quickly moved our LCCA program to the front burner.

We took our finished program to Washington and showed it to the contracting people at USCG Headquarters. The USCG was looking at three large corporate business jets—a Falcon, a Gulfstream and a Challenger. During our time demonstrating our LCCA they asked us to analyze, from a cost point of view, whether they would be better off to buy a new aircraft, a three-year-old used one or a used five-year-old airplane. Bill and I looked smugly at each other, because we knew from our vast experience that the answer would be new. Imagine our astonishment when LCCA showed that one make was best bought new, the second was best bought as a three-year-old aircraft and the third was best bought as a five-year-old used aircraft. So much for our preconceived notions and we realized that we had an excellent new tool to work with. We still keep getting surprising answers from this program. The USCG was our first commercial customer for it.

Each year our basic database business kept growing about 10% each year. After the first year of our partnership, largely through Bill's efforts in the consulting area, our business suddenly jumped about 30% and we realized that we were going to have to have more help. In 1992 we actively started looking for someone to join us. Bill and I both agreed that there was one good prospect that we both knew and had worked with who was technically well qualified. We arranged for him to join us at the National Business Aviation Association convention in Dallas so that we, including our wives, could look him over. Over dinner we discovered that although he was technically well qualified, his primary interests were about medical plans, retirement plans and other benefits. He was already mentally retired.

After dinner we climbed into Bill's car and headed for the de Decker's home in Arlington. We all turned and looked at each other and gave a unanimous thumbs down. This fellow didn't fit the mold of what we wanted on our team, so it was back to the drawing board. Just prior to the convention I had attended a seminar there and had met a professor from Embry-Riddle Aviation University who told me the trouble they were having placing their graduating students. I made the radical suggestion that instead of trying to find an experienced hand, maybe we should take a smart young person and train him ourselves. We all agreed that this was a good idea.

I promptly contacted my recently met professor, told him what we had in mind, and before we knew it, we had 42 resumes on my desk. I duplicated the resumes and sent them to Bill in Texas. Then the next weekend we each went through them and picked—in rank order—the five we liked the best. On Monday we found that we had independently picked the same four out of the five and in the same rank order. The first on our lists was Dave Wyndham and to make a long story short Dave joined us in January of 1993, just in time to help us move into our present office. Dave is an ex-Air Force transport pilot and fits in very well with my background. He is now a full partner in the company. He brings a good operational background to the table and is also a good manager. Today he primarily keeps our databases up to date and manages the production side of our business. He is now our Managing Partner.

Earlier in this narrative I mentioned how Brandon Battles at Bell Helicopters had helped educate me on the real world of helicopter operating costs. After Bill and I joined forces, I discovered that he and Brandon were friends and both were active on the Economics Committee for the Helicopter Association (HAI) in Washington. For some time Brandon had been trying, unsuccessfully, to get Bell's upper management interested in developing a computerized maintenance reporting system for helicopters. Bill looked at, and liked, Brandon's ideas and in October 1995 we added the fourth member to our team. Brandon and Dave are close to the same age and we have a good step down, in age, group. Bill is about twenty years younger than I am and Dave and Brandon are both about twenty years younger than Bill. All four

Partners for over 59 years.

wives are active members of our board of directors and help bring a balanced perspective to our deliberations.

Early in our partnership, we had a call from Jim Van Namee, Manager of Aircraft Procurement for the Federal Aviation Administration in Washington. Jim is a retired Navy officer and the sharpest bureaucrat that I have ever had the pleasure of working with. He is very straightforward and direct to do business with and a real pleasure to work with.

Again it is fascinating to me to see how the Lord works in our lives. In early 1991 Bill took me to the Helicopter Association International convention. During a coffee break at one of the seminars I got chatting with a nice young man named Larry Godwin in the General Services Administration in Washington. I discovered he was very interested in costs for aircraft and, when we started to compare notes, discovered we were talking precisely the same language. It was a language he was having trouble making the government's flight department managers understand.

The upshot of this chance meeting was that Larry invited me to speak at their next Interagency Committee on Aircraft Policy (ICAP) meeting in Washington. This group represents all the aviation department heads for all the civilian agencies in the government—Federal Aviation Administration, FBI, Coast Guard and etc. My assignment was to tell these managers (in polite terms) that they were a bunch of dumb-dumbs when it came to understanding aircraft costs. After this ICAP meeting Larry and I stayed in touch.

Jim Van Namee (Government Aircraft Procurement) also was in contact with Larry Godwin (GSA) and when he mentioned he needed some help with life cycle costs, Larry suggested Conklin & de Decker. Jim called me and told me what he needed. The Navy and Air Force always wanted life cycle costs to be supplied by bidders on equipment. The problem was that the Department of Defense's program was too cumbersome for the Coast Guard to use with their upcoming Request for Proposal. Could we help? We said we could, because we were already working on our own life cycle cost program. We gave Jim a price to develop the information he needed.

A few weeks later Jim called me and was quite insistent on a face-to-face meeting with both Bill and myself. It took a little doing but I finally found a time when we could all three meet in Washington. However, I couldn't figure why it was important to meet face to face. It turned out that the USCG had gotten bids from some other organizations, all of which were significantly higher than ours. Jim liked our proposal, but wanted to know why ours was so low. It was a reality check on our credibility. Bill and I looked at each other and smiled, because we were already working on a life cycle program for ourselves and we had data in hand going back for years. The other guys all had to start from scratch. Jim was greatly relieved and we got the assignment. Until he retired a couple of years ago, Jim was our mentor among many of the government agencies and opened many doors for us. Larry Godwin has also been a big help to us and, today, about one third of our business is with Uncle Sam. And it all began over a free cup of coffee during a break at a seminar.

As I've said before, God is my Instructor Pilot. I'm sure not in charge. All I try to do is be obedient. I endeavor to be a good steward to the gifts I have been given. As Carl Wooton said to me so many tears ago, "If you do the best job you know how to do, the Good Lord will take care of all the rest." That, I think, has been the story of my life